Trout
Stream-Fishing Strategies

MINNETONKA, MINNESOTA

Author Dick Sternberg is not only an avid stream-trout angler, he formerly coordinated the trout and salmon research program for the Minnesota DNR. His trout-fishing adventures have taken him from the wilderness streams of Alaska to the world-class rivers of Argentina.

Trout: Stream-Fishing Strategies

Printed in 2006.

Tom Carpenter
Creative Director

Michele Teigen
Senior Book Development Coordinator

Zachary Marell
Book Design & Production

Gina Germ
Photo Editor

John van Vliet
Fly-Fishing Technical Advisor

Bill Lindner Photography (Bill Lindner, Tom Heck, Brook Martin, Mike Hehner, Jason Lund, Pete Kozad)
Dick Sternberg
Tom Carpenter
Gordon Ellis, Jr.
Mark Emery
Kevin Erb
Scott Ripley
Richard P. Smith
Dave Vedder
Animals, Animals/ ©OSF/L. Milkens, p. 14(a)
Animals, Animals/ ©Carol Geake, p. 14(b)
Animals, Animals/ ©Donald Specker, p. 14(c)
Animals, Animals/ ©Bill Beatty, p. 15(b,f)
Animals, Animals/ ©Ed Degginger, p. 15(c)
Animals, Animals/ ©G.I. Bernard/OSF, p. 15(d)
Animals, Animals/ ©Mark Stouffer Enterprises, p. 23(a,c)
Animals, Animals/ ©Breck Kent, p. 23(b)
Photography

Special thanks to Pierre, somewhere in Argentina, who allowed us to use his sea trout photograph.

Dave Schelitzche
Joe Tomelleri, pp. 25,27,29,33,35,38,39,41,43,49
Maynard Reece, pp. 39,45,47
Illustration

9 10 11 12 13 / 09 08 07 06 05

© 1999 North American Fishing Club

ISBN 1-58159-036-9

North American Fishing Club
12301 Whitewater Drive
Minnetonka, MN 55343
www.fishingclub.com

INTRODUCTION

Mystique surrounds trout and trout fishing. Maybe its the fishes' wary nature; maybe it's the places trout fishing takes us—from pretty little streams just out our back door to classic streams and rivers across our country and possibly the world. Maybe we just like surrounding the sport with misty uneasiness.

Mystique.

Let's be honest. If you look at trout fishing through eyes not clouded by tradition, you'll find a fishery that offers opportunities for all anglers. That's why *Trout: Stream-Fishing Strategies* looks at techniques, flies, baits and lures that catch trout, and doesn't focus on one method or type of tackle.

There are no hidden secrets to catching trout. Sure, it can be a challenge at times, and that's just one of the reasons we come back. But I've found that if an angler hits the water equipped with knowledge and a game plan, the game is just that much more fun.

You don't need a fly rod or box full of feathered hooks to learn from this book. Yet if you do fly fish or plan to start, there's plenty here to expand your strategies, skills and techniques. That's true for fans of spinning gear as well. Trout are equal-opportunity fish!

And in the end, that's what it's all about—getting out to the beautiful places trout call home. Good reading, and good fishing. See you on the stream!

Steve Pennaz

Executive Director
North American Fishing Club

CONTENTS

Introduction   2

The Fish   **4**

   Trout Basics   6

   Spawning Habits   20

   Rainbow Trout   24

   Brown Trout   28

   Brook Trout   32

   Cutthroat Trout   36

   Golden Trout   40

   Bull Trout   42

   Dolly Varden   44

   Arctic Char   46

   Arctic Grayling   48

The Waters   **50**

   Trout Habitat   52

   How to "Read" the Water   62

The Gear   **66**

   Rods & Reels   68

   Line   74

Waders & Hip Boots   78

Boats & Motors   80

Accessories   82

Stream-Fishing Techniques   **86**

   A Stealthy Approach   88

   Fishing with Hardware   90

   Jig Fishing   100

   Fishing with Natural Bait   102

   Fly Fishing   118

   Releasing Trout   140

Out of the Ordinary   **142**

   Fishing Big Water   144

   Fishing Tight Spots   148

   Trophy Fishing   150

Index   154

THE FISH

*T*he key to catching stream trout is learning the habits of each species; then you can tailor your methods accordingly.

Trout: Stream-Fishing Strategies

TROUT BASICS

More books have been written on trout fishing than on all other types of fishing combined. Some dedicated anglers have libraries consisting of hundreds of books on every imaginable trout-related subject—including not only the equipment, skills and techniques involved with the sport, but also the history and romance surrounding it.

Part of trout fishing's allure is the mysterious nature of the fish. You could easily walk a mile of a "blue-ribbon" trout stream without ever seeing a trout. The fish are masters of concealment: hiding under the bank, in the roots of a fallen tree or in the turbulent water behind a boulder. Even when they venture into the open, their camouflage makes them nearly impossible to see in the rippling water.

And you can't help but be awestruck by a trout's stunning beauty. Whether it's the yellow-orange flanks and crimson spots of a brown trout or the silvery sides and pinkish lateral band of a rainbow, every species of stream trout has its own unique appeal.

And then there's the challenge of making the fish bite. Although there are times when stream trout will eagerly strike practically any lure or bait that comes within sight, more often they are highly cautious, testing the skill of even the veteran angler.

Fly fishermen, for example, must convince the trout that a bit of fur or feathers resembles something in the fish's diet. It's not just a matter of selecting the right fly; it's learning to present the fly so it looks like real food.

Adding to the appeal of the fish themselves is the beauty of the country in which they live. An unspoiled trout stream has a certain magical charm that keeps an angler coming back—often for an entire lifetime.

For pure beauty, few other freshwater gamefish can compare to a trout.

Although trout have legions of devotees, many anglers are so intimidated by what they read about trout fishing that they never take up the sport.

They believe, for example, that trout are the smartest fish that swim and only an expert can tempt them to bite.

It is certainly true that trout are extremely wary. They have to be; otherwise they would be easy targets for predators including larger fish and fish-eating birds. But there is no evidence that they are any more intelligent than most other kinds of freshwater fish.

So don't be put off by all of the "superfish" hype; you'll catch your share of trout if you take the time to learn their habits and their habitat preferences.

Before we go into detail, however, here are a few basic things you should know:

•Trout are members of the salmon family (*Salmonidae*), which also includes Pacific and Atlantic salmon, grayling and whitefish.

•Trout are sometimes divided into two categories: true trout and *chars*. True trout, such as rainbows and browns, have a light background coloration with dark

spots. Chars, such as brook trout and Arctic char, have a dark background with lighter spots. (See photos.)

•The majority of trout require relatively cold water, from 50 to 70°F. As a result, streams must be fed by springs or snowmelt, or they must be at a northerly latitude or high altitude in order to support trout year round.

•Chars generally need colder water than true trout. A bull trout, for instance, prefers water around 50°F while a brown is comfortable in water approaching 70 and can tolerate water in the upper 70s.

The rainbow trout (top) is a true trout; the brook trout (bottom) is a char.

• Most trout species require moving water to spawn successfully. These fish are referred to as "stream trout." Many stream trout species, however, are also capable of living in lakes—but they must either be stocked or have access to a spawning stream.

• Many species of trout have *anadromous* forms that spend most of their life at sea or in the open water of large inland lakes and then return to tributary streams to spawn. Anadromous forms are usually larger, sleeker and more silvery than their freshwater counterparts.

• The table quality of most trout species is excellent, but catch-and-release fishing is now encouraged in most heavily fished waters; in many, catch-and-release is mandatory.

• Characteristics of individual trout species vary tremendously. There are major differences in temperature preferences as well as in food habits, spawning behavior and even

fighting qualities. A rainbow, for example, is a noted leaper while a brook trout tends to fight deep. We will explore these differences more thoroughly on pages 20-49.

Most trout are exceptionally strong fighters and some, like the rainbow, are remarkable leapers.

TROUT SENSES

Observant anglers can learn a great deal about how trout use their senses to find food and avoid predators. For example, it's obvious that trout have excellent vision, because they are quickly "put down" by any sudden movement. Once spooked, they are nearly impossible to catch for a considerable time.

Savvy trout anglers understand the importance of keeping low to stay out of the trout's "window" of vision. Because of the way light rays entering the water are bent, trout can see a much wider area above the surface than you would expect (lower right).

The trout's keen vision is evident to any fly fisherman who has been frustrated because his fly was not the same size or color as that of the insect on which the trout were feeding.

A trout's color-vision capability is also apparent to anglers who use "hardware." There are times, for instance, when the fish ignore a plain silver spoon. But if you attach a small piece of fluorescent orange tape, they greedily attack it.

Anglers walking the bank of a trout stream know that a heavy footstep has pretty much the same effect on trout as a sudden movement. Trout detect the vibrations using their well-developed lateral-line sense, consisting of a network of sensitive nerve endings along their side.

The fact that trout have a good sense of smell is evident if you watch how they react to an odor-producing bait such as fresh salmon eggs. The eggs emit a milky colored scent trail, which the trout quickly detect and follow to the source.

Trout have a keen sense of smell, as evidenced by their ability to quickly home in on smelly baits such as salmon eggs or "trout candy."

Understanding a Trout's Window of Vision

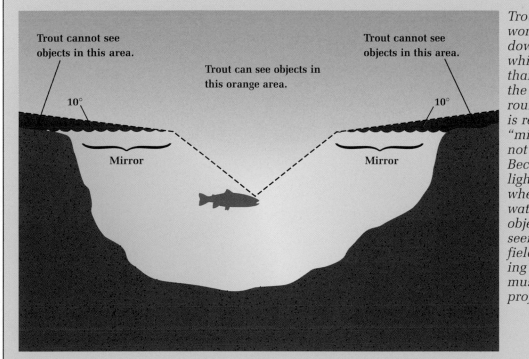

Trout cannot see objects in this area.

Trout can see objects in this orange area.

Trout cannot see objects in this area.

10°

Mirror

10°

Mirror

Trout view the outside world through a window, the diameter of which is a little more than twice the depth of the fish. The area surrounding the window is referred to as a "mirror"; the fish cannot see through it. Because of the way light rays are bent when they enter the water, trout can see objects that would seem to be out of the field of view, explaining why an angler must keep a very low profile.

FOOD HABITS

Judging by the number of books that have been written on "matching the hatch," you would think all trout are highly selective eaters that turn their noses up at anything but the specific insect that happens to be hatching on a given day.

While it's true that trout can be quite selective during a heavy insect hatch, that behavior is the exception rather than the rule. If you examine the stomach contents of a trout, you're likely to find a variety of insect life as well as some small fish, a few crustaceans and maybe even some fish eggs, a mouse, a frog or a nightcrawler.

There are considerable differences in selectivity between species. Browns are generally regarded as the most selective; brook trout and cutthroat, the least. Trout are rarely selective when they're feeding on insects below the surface.

Even when trout are feeding selectively on a certain insect, you don't need a fly that is a perfect match for the natural. You can usually tempt the fish to take a fly of the approximate size, shape and color.

Trout feed on practically any kind of insect, including adult and juvenile forms of aquatic and terrestrial species. Insects are a mainstay for trout of all ages, but they're most important to young trout. As trout grow older, they begin to consume more fish.

As a rule, the larger the percentage of fish in the diet, the faster trout grow and the greater their maximum size. It's not unusual for brown trout in a "minnow stream" to exceed the 10-pound mark.

But in an "insect stream," a 2 pounder would cause a stir.

Although fish are an important component in the diet of practically all large trout, some species are more fish-oriented than others. Good-sized bull trout, Dolly Varden and brown trout, for example, feed on fish almost exclusively.

The fish-eating habits of Dolly Varden have given the species a bad name. In fact,

Alaska once offered a bounty on Dollies, and fishermen were allowed to take them by practically any means, including explosives. While it's true that Dollies commonly feed on the eggs and young of other trout and salmon, so do many other salmonid species. In fact, most salmonids do not hesitate to eat their own kind.

Books may be available to help you identify the insects common to streams in your region.

On the pages that follow, you'll learn how to identify some of the most common trout foods. We'll also show you how to determine what food types are most common in the streams that you fish.

Aquatic Insects

Hungry trout will eat almost any kind of insect, but aquatic species comprise the largest part of their diet. And of those aquatic types, immature forms are much more prevalent than adults. This is not surprising considering that immatures are available to the trout year round, while adults appear for only a few days following a hatch.

Most immature insects are consumed as they drift with the current. Trout take cover in a spot that affords them protection from the current; they quickly dart out to grab a drifting insect and then return to their lie.

Knowledgeable anglers are constantly on the lookout for a significant insect hatch, but they also know when the heaviest drift cycles occur (usually late in the day) and plan their fishing accordingly.

Trout feed mainly on the following four major groups of aquatic insects. Each group is represented by hundreds of different species.

*Mayflies (*Ephemeroptera*)*

Mayflies, one of the most common aquatic insects, generally have a one-year life cycle. The majority of their life is spent as a nymph (top), which is easily identified by a single pair of wingpads, gills on the abdomen and two or three long tail filaments. When a nymph is ready to hatch, it swims to the surface and emerges as a "dun" (middle), which has cloudy, upright wings that are usually grayish or brownish. Because duns float on the surface as their wings dry, they are a favorite trout food. When their wings are dry, duns fly to trees and bushes along the stream, where they soon transform into a "spinner" (bottom), which is a sexually mature adult. Spinners have clearer wings, brighter colors and longer tail filaments than duns.

Stoneflies (Plecoptera)

Stoneflies require cold, clean water, so they are less common than mayflies. A stonefly nymph (left) has two pairs of wingpads, two short, thick tail filaments and gills on the underside of its thorax. The nymphal stage lasts from one to four years, depending on the species. Adults (right) are dull brownish or grayish and their wings lie flat rather than stand upright.

Caddisflies (Trichoptera)

Caddisflies are abundant in the majority of trout streams. The larvae, which are usually tan or cream-colored, have a segmented body with three pairs of legs near the front. Most types live in a case made of sand or sticks (left), but some do not build cases. When they're about a year old, the larvae seal themselves into the cases and begin to pupate, developing wingpads and legs. Soon they emerge as adults (right), which are brownish and have tentlike wings.

Midges (Diptera)

Midges, found in most trout waters, are generally smaller than other aquatic insects and inhabit slow-moving, weedy portions of streams. The larvae (left) are slender and vary greatly in color, but most are brownish or reddish. The latter are sometimes called "bloodworms." At an age of only a few months, the larvae pupate and then hatch into long-legged adults (right), which often resemble overgrown mosquitoes.

Common Baitfish

Chubs (genus Hybopsis) rank among the most abundant stream-dwelling baitfish in North America. Creek chubs and hornyhead chubs, also called redtail chubs (shown) are most common. Chubs differ from dace (below) in that chubs have a groove between the upper lip and the snout.

Dace (genus Phoxinus and Rhinichthys) are found primarily in small streams, but some species live in bogs and lakes. The blacknose dace (shown) thrives in fast water. In dace, the groove on the upper lip does not continue around the snout.

Shiners (genus Notropis) are common both in lakes and streams throughout North America. They are easy to identify because of their silvery sides. The common shiner (shown) has a deeper body and larger scales than most other shiner species.

Sculpins (genus Cottus) live under rocks in fast-flowing streams. The mottled sculpin (shown) is the most common species. Sculpins are easy to identify because of their large head, scaleless body and huge pectoral fins, which they use to rest comfortably on the bottom.

Other Trout Foods

Scuds (sometimes called freshwater shrimp) resemble immature aquatic insects, but they are really crustaceans. They are normally found in slow-moving stream stretches, usually clinging to vegetation. Scuds may be pink, orange, olive, tan or even bluish.

Crayfish, a favorite food of good-sized trout, are commonly found on a rocky or weedy bottom with light to moderate current. They have four sets of legs and a pair of large pincers, which they use for catching food and defending themselves. Crayfish are usually brownish to olive in color, but they may be reddish or bluish.

Terrestrial insects such as grasshoppers (shown), crickets, beetles and ants, commonly fall or are blown into streams where they are quickly eaten by trout. Even when trout are gorging themselves on aquatic insects, they seldom hesitate to take a terrestrial.

Leeches cling to rocks, sticks or weeds, usually in areas of slow-moving current. When they detach themselves to feed, leeches swim with an undulating wiggle that trout find hard to resist. Leeches are usually black, brown or olive, sometimes with stripes or mottling.

How to Determine What Trout are Eating

As explained earlier, it's not always necessary to precisely match the hatch, but a little knowledge of the most prevalent foods goes a long way toward making an intelligent lure selection.

The only way to be certain what trout have been eating is to catch one and check its stomach contents. The problem is, if you're able to catch one, you already know what kind of lure it's willing to take. And if you don't know how to properly use a stomach pump (opposite), you could kill the fish.

Trout are opportunists, always ready to take advantage of whatever foods are most abundant. So you can get a pretty good idea of what trout are eating by checking food abundance in the stream. You can accomplish this in several ways—by turning over rocks or logs, sifting through clumps of vegetation or seining.

Another method of determining what insects are hatching is to check a "hatch chart" for the region in which you are fishing. Actual hatch dates of various insects, however, may vary by a week or two from what the chart shows. It's a good idea to keep your own records on hatch dates for your favorite streams.

When a heavy insect hatch is in progress, the primary food may seem to be apparent. But that is not necessarily the case. There will be times, for example, when big mayflies are hatching all around you and you see numerous rises. Assuming the trout are feeding on mayfly duns, you tie on a large mayfly imitation. When the fish repeatedly refuse your offering, you finally notice that they're actually feeding on tiny midges, not mayflies.

The easiest way to determine what insects trout are eating is to turn over some rocks to see what kinds of immature insects are most numerous. Not all immatures cling to rocks, but many types do.

Check the stomach contents of your catch using a stomach pump. Insert the suction tube gently so you don't damage the stomach wall.

Sift through clumps of weeds to see what kinds of insects are clinging to the vegetation. You're likely to find scuds among the weeds, as well.

To make a seine, attach screen or fine-mesh netting between a pair of sticks. While someone holds the seine on the bottom, another person dislodges rocks and roots up from the bottom just upstream, causing bottom organisms to drift into the net.

Consult a hatch chart to get an idea of when certain kinds of insects will be hatching in your area. (Detailed charts are usually available at local fly shops.) Then start your own hatch charts for streams you fish.

SPAWNING HABITS

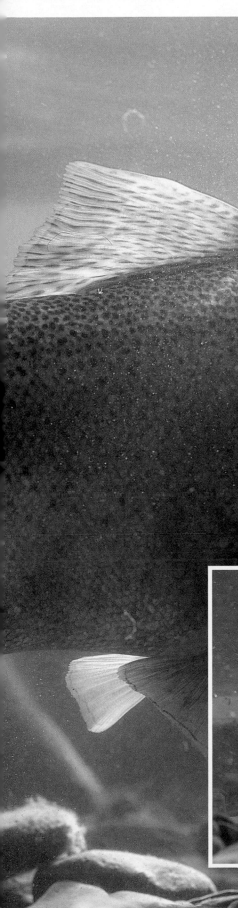

Trout spawning habits are variable and complex. As evidenced by the chart on the next page, different trout species spawn at different times, at different water temperatures and in different types of habitat.

But practically all trout require flowing water to spawn successfully. They dig redds, or nests, in which the eggs are buried. Water flowing through the gravel keeps the eggs aerated.

In some instances, brook trout can spawn successfully in lakes, but only in areas with upwelling springs. Grayling differ from most other salmonids in that they deposit their eggs on top of the gravel, rather than excavating a redd.

Prior to spawning, male trout exhibit some remarkable physical changes. Their jaws grow longer and the lower jaw often develops a pro-

nounced hook, called a *kype*. Their color becomes more vivid and often much darker.

The female excavates the redd by turning on her side and beating the bottom with her tail to remove the gravel to make a depression for the eggs (below). As a rule, the redd is a little longer than her body and several inches deep. Often, a female digs several redds and deposits eggs in each of them.

During redd construction, the male stands by, defending his territory against smaller males. If the intruders get too close, the dominant male nips them with his kype to drive them off.

When the pair is ready to spawn, they hold side by side. With their bodies rigid, backs arched and mouths agape, they vibrate violently to release the eggs and milt into the redd.

Female trout digging a redd.

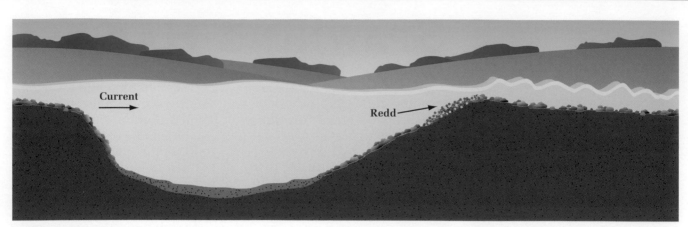

Current

Redd

A trout often constructs its redd in the tail of a pool, because that is the most favorable spot for egg survival. Because of the sloping bottom here, water is forced through the gravel, keeping the eggs aerated.

Trout eggs are quite large compared to those of most warmwater and coolwater fish species. Brook trout eggs, for example, may be up to 5 millimeters in diameter, compared to only 1.5 millimeters for largemouth bass eggs. Consequently, a large trout deposits only about 5,000 eggs, while a large bass may deposit 10 times that many.

If the bottom of a stream is too silty, trout will not be able to spawn successfully. The fine particles cover the eggs, preventing them from getting sufficient oxygen.

This explains why fisheries managers do everything possible to stabilize stream banks and prevent erosion.

Streams that do not have natural reproduction may still hold excellent trout populations, but the fish must be stocked.

When and Where Trout Spawn

Species	Spawning Time; Water Temperature	Spawning Habitat
Brook trout	Fall; 40-49°F	Headwaters area, usually around large springs
Brown trout	Fall; 44-49°F	Headwaters of stream and small tributaries
Rainbow trout	Spring; 50-59°F	Tails of pools and small tributaries
Cutthroat trout	Early spring; 43-48°F	Very small tributaries
Golden trout	Summer; 48-53°F	Tails of pools, either in the stream itself or in tributaries
Bull trout	Early fall; 45-50°F	Tributaries
Dolly Varden	Fall; 40-46°F	Main channel of good-sized stream
Arctic char	Fall; 37-42°F	Slow-moving pools
Grayling	Early spring; 43-49°F	Small tributaries

Stages of the Spawning Cycle

1 Trout deposit eggs in a redd. The eggs incubate there for one to five months, depending on the species. If the eggs are deposited in the fall, they incubate through the winter and then hatch in spring. If the eggs are deposited in spring, they hatch by summer. Eggs that are not buried deep enough in the redd will be consumed by predators such as crayfish, giant water beetles and fish. Severe floods can also destroy a redd. Fisheries managers sometimes choose the variety of trout they stock based on when it spawns. If they know, for example, that floods usually occur in March, they can select a variety of trout that spawns in April, after floodwaters have subsided.

2 After the eggs hatch, the fry remain in the gravel and get their food from a yolk sac, which remains attached to their body. Within a few weeks, the fry are strong enough to wiggle out of the gravel and begin feeding on their own. The yolk sac has now been completely absorbed and they begin to feed on plankton. Predation is particularly severe at this early life stage. On the average, only one fry in a hundred will survive to age one.

3 By the time the fish are a few inches long, a row of dark vertical bars is apparent along the sides of their body. The fish are now called parr, and the bars are called parr marks. The parr marks usually disappear within the first year or two, but some trout retain them until adulthood. Golden trout never lose their parr marks.

4 Anadromous trout, such as steelhead, have yet another life stage. The young may spend two or three years in the spawning stream before migrating to the sea or to a large inland lake. As they begin to develop the migratory urge, their color changes to a brilliant silver, the parr marks disappear and the fish, now called smolts, start to work their way downstream.

RAINBOW TROUT

Strong, beautiful and acrobatic, the rainbow trout is considered by many to be the perfect sportfish. It inhabits pure waters—often in beautiful settings—but it can also be found in streams that would seem better suited for carp and bullheads.

Catching rainbows consistently requires skill, but not the degree of skill required to take the wily brown trout.

The rainbow is indigenous to North America, with a native range extending from northern Mexico into Alaska. Thanks to widespread stocking, you can now catch rainbows throughout most of the continent.

Rainbows are found in unlikely places such as North Dakota, fee-fishing ponds in the outskirts of Cleveland or put-and-take lakes in Florida. More rainbows are taken by anglers than any other species of trout, and no other fish is raised and stocked as extensively throughout the world, including New Zealand, northern India, South Africa, Europe, Chile, Argentina and Japan.

There are two recognized subspecies of rainbow trout: the red-band rainbow, by far the most common, and the steelhead, the migratory form found mainly in coastal streams and in the Great Lakes and its tributaries.

But within these subspecies are more than 100 distinct strains, or varieties, each offering slightly different qualities. Some of the more common strains include Eagle Lake, Arlee, Kamloops, Shasta, Kern River, Royal Silver, Donaldson and Skamania.

The majority of rainbows spawn in spring, usually from February through June. Like most other trout, they build their redds in the gravel at the tail of a pool or in tributary streams.

Rainbow trout commonly hybridize with other salmonids, primarily cutthroat and golden trout. In fact, rainbows in some waters are difficult to distinguish from cutthroats. But if you examine the two closely, you'll see that the cutthroat has a patch of teeth on the back of its tongue and the rainbow does not.

Rainbows grow to exceptional size. One weighing 52 pounds was once taken in Jewel Lake, British Columbia. The official world record is 42 pounds, 2 ounces. The fish (a steelhead) was taken in Bell Island, Alaska, in 1970.

The life span of a rainbow may be as long as 12 years, depending on the location.

Red-band rainbows (Oncorhynchus mykiss gairdneri) *get their name from the reddish to pinkish band on their sides. The coloration of the gill plates usually matches that of the lateral band. The back can be anywhere from green to blue to olive-brown, with numerous black spots. The flanks are usually silvery, the belly is white and the tail features radiating rows of black spots. Stream-dwelling rainbows tend to have more intense colors and heavier spotting than lake dwellers.*

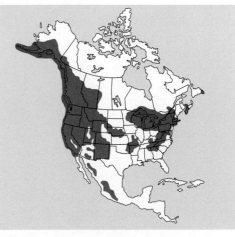

Rainbow trout range.

On the average, a 2-year-old rainbow is about 8 or 9 inches long, but some fast-growing strains, such as the Donaldson, put on as much as an inch per month for the first 2 years of life, reaching a weight of 7 pounds in that time.

Rainbows prefer the fast-moving stretches of rivers, but they're also at home in spring-fed creeks and in cold-water lakes, ponds and reservoirs.

There is not a more acrobatic fish in fresh water than a rainbow taken in fast current. When a good-sized "bow" grabs your fly or lure, it immediately starts to tail-walk and sizzle line off your reel. Before you know it, you're checking your spool to see if you have enough line.

STEELHEAD

For countless West Coast and Great Lakes anglers, there is only one sportfish worthy of their attention—the steelhead. This migratory form of rainbow is an awe-inspiring fish, combining the rainbow's leaping ability with the strength and power of a salmon.

Unlike Pacific salmon, which return to their spawning stream only once and then die after the eggs are deposited, steelhead may live to spawn several times.

Steelhead are silvery when they first enter the rivers, but as they move upstream and near their spawning grounds, their color begins to darken, their reddish band appears and the male develops a kype.

On their way to the spawning grounds, steelhead leap raging waterfalls that would appear to be impassable. It's not unusual to see them hurdling a six-foot falls, and

The leaping ability of the steelhead is legendary.

they can negotiate much higher ones, assuming there are a series of step-pools along the way.

Whether or not steelhead feed once they enter their spawning stream is a subject of considerable debate. The fish can be caught, but many anglers believe they bite out of reflex or territoriality. Often, you have to drift a bait past them repeatedly to draw a strike.

To catch steelhead consistently, you must be in the right place at the right time. If you're fishing the upstream

reach of a river during the early part of the run, for example, you probably won't see a steelhead. The same will happen if you're fishing the downstream reach toward the end of the run.

Summer vs. Winter Runs

Steelhead that enter coastal rivers in spring, summer and fall are known as summer-run. Those entering in late fall, winter and early spring are known as winter-run. On most rivers these two strains

*Steelhead (*Oncorhynchus mykiss irideus*) resemble ordinary rainbows except that they are sleeker and more silvery. The fish grow large, averaging 6 to 12 pounds. In the rushing, isolated rivers of British Columbia, steelhead may reach weights in excess of 25 pounds.*

Steelhead range.

will spawn at approximately the same time, in late winter or early spring.

Winter-run fish are generally the biggest, although summer-run fish may reach 20 pounds. The largest steelhead tend to appear in rivers at the end of a given run.

In many Great Lakes tributaries, steelhead enter the streams in fall on what some biologists call a "mock spawning run." Although no spawning actually takes place, the fall run gives anglers a good shot at catching a trophy steelhead.

The main difference between fishing for steelhead on the Pacific Coast and along the Great Lakes is the size of the stream. Not all coastal rivers are huge but some, like the Columbia, are a mile across in some spots.

Midwestern streams are generally much smaller. Many Lake Michigan tributaries, for example, are no more than 25 feet wide and a couple feet deep, but they have good runs of fish approaching 20 pounds.

On male rainbows, the cheeks and lateral band turn dark pink at spawning time.

BROWN TROUT

Considered "the thinking man's trout" because of their ability to outwit most anglers, brown trout were widely introduced into North America in the late 1800s. They were to provide a substitute for the easy-to-catch brook trout, which were rapidly disappearing as a result of fishing pressure and civilization's encroachment on their cold, clear streams.

Browns are native to Europe and the British Isles. In fact, they are sometimes called German browns, or Loch Leven trout in reference to a lake of that name in Scotland. The fish have also been introduced into Asia, New Zealand, South America and Africa. Next to rainbows, browns are the most widely distributed trout in the world.

Early taxonomists recognized many subspecies of

brown trout, but widespread stocking has led to so much genetic mixing that these forms can no longer be distinguished. Today, there are no officially recognized brown trout subspecies.

Brown trout sometimes hybridize with brook trout to produce "tiger trout," which get their name from the distinct black and yellow markings on their side. Tiger trout have an aggressive disposition and are considerably easier to catch than pure browns.

The biggest browns usually come from lakes, but the world record, weighing 40 pounds, 4 ounces, was caught in the Little Red River, Arkansas, in 1992. In most trout streams, a 5 pounder is a trophy and in heavily fished eastern streams, a 2 pounder is considered good-sized.

Brown trout (Salmo trutta), above, have brownish sides that dissolve into yellow toward the belly. The sides have numerous dark spots and a few red spots, some of which have whitish to bluish halos. The tail is unspotted or has only a few indistinct spots.

Tiger trout.

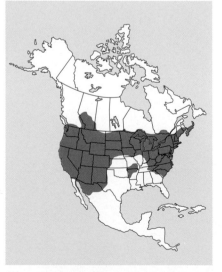

Brown trout range.

A typical Great Lakes "Football."

Spawning male brown trout.

Brown trout are fall spawners. When the water temperature drops to the mid-40s, they begin building their redds in the upper reaches of a stream or in small tributaries. The eggs incubate over the winter and hatch in spring.

At spawning time, the Male's yellowish coloration becomes much more intense, sometimes changing to bright orange. A strong kype develops on the lower jaw and the lower fins turn charcoal-colored.

Browns may live as long as 18 years, but their usual life span is 9 years or less. Their growth rate is highly variable, depending on the type of water and the food supply. In an average trout stream, the fish usually reach 18 inches by the sixth year.

Lake-dwelling brown trout, such as those in some of the Great Lakes, are much heavier for their length than stream browns. In fact, Great Lakes browns have such deep bodies that they're often called "footballs."

Like most other trout, browns feed heavily on aquatic insects such as mayflies, caddisflies and stoneflies, as well as a variety of terrestrials. But large brown trout are primarily fish eaters and sometimes turn cannibalistic. In fact, if a body of water has too many big browns, stocking other trout may be fruitless because they're quickly eaten. Big browns also love crayfish.

Browns can stand up to heavy fishing pressure better than most other trout species. There is no evidence to indicate they're any more "intelligent" than other trout; their habits simply make it more difficult for anglers to catch them consistently.

Trout: Stream-Fishing Strategies

For example, browns tend to be nocturnal feeders, and many of the largest fish are taken after dark. During the day, the fish often hole up in the heaviest cover where it's nearly impossible to put a fly or lure.

More than any other trout, browns seek cover that offers overhead protection. They're much less likely to feed in the open than are rainbows and cutthroat.

You may see browns rising during a heavy insect hatch, but they usually base their feeding activity from a partic-ular feeding station, or *lie.* Unlike other trout species, you'll seldom see browns cruising about at random, sip-ping insects off the surface.

Compared to other stream trout, browns can tolerate slightly warmer water. They prefer water temperatures in the upper 50s to low 60s and can survive for short periods at water temperatures near 80°F. They also seem to be more tolerant of muddy water and even pollution. In the upper Clark's Fork River in western Montana, for exam-ple, trout thrive despite heavy concentrations of toxic metals accumulated from decades of mining activity.

Browns are less acrobatic than rainbows and generally wage a determined battle in deep water. But it's not unusual for them to jump once or twice when first hooked.

Sea Trout

The anadromous form of the brown trout, called the sea trout, enters coastal rivers to spawn. A few sea trout are taken in streams along the U.S. east coast, where they average about 5 pounds. But the majority of sea trout are caught in the coastal streams of Argentina, Chile, New Zealand and Europe.

Known for their awe-inspiring leaps and siz-zling runs, sea trout are sil-very in appearance when they first return from the ocean. But they gradually darken and take on the look of a freshwater brown as they spend more time in their spawning rivers.

Most sea trout spend the first three years of life in their home rivers before migrating to the sea. Some individuals return to their home streams after only a few months; oth-ers remain at sea for up to three years. The longer the fish stay at sea, the larger they are when they return.

An Argentina sea trout.

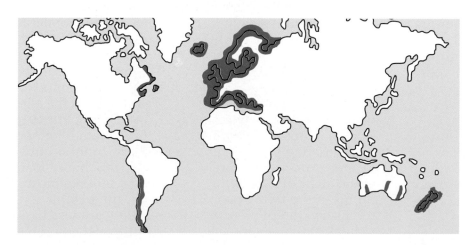

Sea trout range.

BROOK TROUT

Arguably the most beautiful of all trout, the brook trout is a true North American native. Originally found from northern Georgia to the Arctic Circle, it has now been stocked throughout the western states, in the western provinces of Canada and in Alaska. Brookies have also been introduced into Europe, Australia and South America.

Brook trout, also called speckled trout, don't reach the size of the other major stream trout species; but brookies are enthusiastic biters and their table quality is unequalled.

These two qualities, however, have contributed to their decline throughout much of their native range. Anyone can catch a brook trout simply by dangling a worm in the water. And when a brookie gets caught, it's likely to wind up in the frying pan.

Because of their vulnerability to hook and line, brookies reach the largest size in remote waters. The premier North American brook trout streams are in Labrador and Ontario. The world-record brookie, weighing 14 pounds, 9 ounces, was caught in the Nipigon River, Ontario, in 1916.

Considered "opportunistic" feeders, brook trout will eat pretty much any food that is available. Like most other trout, their staple is insects, but they are less likely to take adult insects on the surface.

This explains why most fly fishermen pursue brookies using nymphs, streamers or wet flies. Brookies are also fond of worms and leeches, and will sometimes consume snails, frogs, mice, fish eggs, and small fish. But they are less fish-oriented than most other trout. Their willingness to take practically any food also helps explain their susceptibility to angling.

Brook trout belong to the genus *Salvelinus*, which are referred to as char. Other members of the group include Arctic char, Dolly Varden, lake trout and bull trout. These species require colder water than other types of trout. The brook trout's preferred temperature range is 52 to 56°F, although they can survive in waters approaching 70.

The brookie's liking for cold water makes it easy for savvy anglers to locate them. They're typically found in the headwaters area of a stream, where spring flow keeps the water temperature cold enough. Farther down the stream, brook trout are usually scarce, but you may find a few in pockets below cold tributaries or around upwelling springs in the main channel.

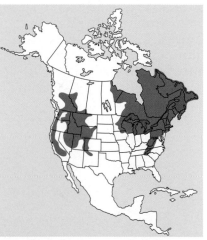

Brook trout range.

*Brook trout (*Salvelinus fontinalis*) have green-black backs with lighter, wormlike markings. The sides feature pale spots and a few red spots with bluish halos. The lower half of the body grades from greenish to yellowish to orange, often with a black streak on the belly. The lower fins have distinct white leading edges. The tail is almost square, accounting for the common name "squaretail."*

Unfortunately, deforestation, overgrazing, stream channelization and dam building have greatly reduced the amount of cold, clear water available for brook trout. The warmer, murkier water is better suited for browns and rainbows, if it can support trout at all.

Brook trout are fall spawners. Spawning activity peaks in September in the northern part of their range and in December in the southern part. The female digs a redd in the headwaters of a stream or in a very small tributary, often around upwelling springs. Unlike other stream trout, brookies are also capable of spawning successfully in lakes if there are areas of good spring flow.

Male brook trout can be crossed with

Splake have light wormlike markings on the back and light spots on the sides. The tail is more deeply forked than that of a brook trout.

female lake trout to produce *splake* (s̲p̲eckled X la̲k̲e), which are most commonly stocked in a lake environment. As discussed earlier, brookies are also crossed with brown trout to produce tiger trout (p. 29). In the West, brook trout hybridize naturally with bull trout, a phenomenon

that has contributed to the decline of pure-strain bulls.

Brook trout may live 10 years or more, but fish older than 6 are rare. They grow quite slowly; on the average, a 6-year-old brookie is about 16 inches long. They grow even more slowly in waters that are warmer than what they prefer.

Spawning male brook trout develop colors that are extremely intense. The red spots and blue halos become much more prominent, as does the orange coloration on the undersides. The white leading edges on the lower fins are accentuated by a black band, and the lower jaw develops a slight kype.

Trout: Stream-Fishing Strategies

Salters & Coasters

The sea-going form of brook trout, called the *salter*, is most common along the east coast of Canada, particularly in New Brunswick and Prince Edward Island. Salters are also known as sea trout, the same name used for sea-run browns (p. 31).

In years past, the Great Lakes (particularly Lake Superior) held large numbers of anadromous brook trout, called *coasters*, which closely resemble salters. It's rare to catch a coaster today, but some natural resources agencies in the Great Lakes region are attempting to reestablish them. Wildlife Forever is assisting in the recovery effort.

Coasters (shown) and salters tend to be more silvery than their inland counterparts, and their spotting is less distinct.

The brook trout's cooperative nature makes it an easy target for most anglers. Many conservation agencies now use size limits or no-kill regulations to protect brookies in heavily fished waters.

CUTTHROAT TROUT

Cutthroat are natives of the North American West, named for the reddish or orange slash marks or "cuts" on the lower jaw.

When you hold a cutthroat in your hand and see the flaming red slash marks on the throat, you'll know immediately where the species got its name.

Biologists recognize many subspecies of cutthroat trout, all of which are found in the western United States, western Canada and Alaska. The most common subspecies are the Yellowstone, West Slope, Lahontan and Coastal (p. 38).

Adding to the confusion in identifying cutthroats is the fact that they commonly hybridize with rainbow and golden trout. Hybrids are so common in some waters that even trained biologists have a hard time making an accurate identification.

Cutthroat favor water temperatures from 55 to 62°F—about the same range as favored by rainbow. The habitat preferences of the two are quite similar. Like rainbows, cutthroat are equally at home in still or moving water, but they do not spawn successfully in a lake environment. Rainbows, however, will tolerate swifter current.

Cutthroat are quite sensitive to disruptions in their environment. The West Slope cutthroat, for example, has disappeared from all but a few of its native streams in Montana because of logging operations and stocking of rainbows. Attempts are being made to restore degraded streams so the fish can be reintroduced.

Many anglers would argue that cutthroat are even less discriminating in their choice of food than brook trout. Brookies are prone to subsurface feeding, while cutthroat may feed on the surface or anywhere in the water column. Their opportunistic food habits explain why they're considered one of the easiest trout to catch.

The cutthroat's high vulnerability to angling, combined with its tendency to interbreed with rainbows, explains why it has not been widely stocked outside of its native range.

Cutthroat are spring spawners, although coastal cutthroat usually begin to spawn in late-winter. Most spawning takes place in small tributary streams. An individual cutthroat may spawn only in alternate years.

Although cutthroat may live as long as 9 years, a normal life span is 4 to 7. The growth rate is highly variable, depending on subspecies and altitude.

In 6 years, a West Slope cutthroat

grows only to about 15 inches; a Lahontan, 24 inches. The world-record cutthroat (a Lahontan) weighed 41 pounds. It was taken in Pyramid Lake, Nevada, in 1925. In a high-mountain stream, a 12-inch cutthroat is a trophy.

Cutthroat are not as acrobatic as rainbow; a hooked fish usually wages a strong subsurface struggle. But the breathtaking scenery of cutthroat country more than compensates for any shortcomings on the end of the line.

Spawning male cutthroat develop a red patch on the side of the head and a red lateral band, much like that of a rainbow. The yellowish coloration on the flanks becomes more intense. There is no prominent kype.

Coastal Cutthroat

Sea-run cutthroat trout are called coastal cutthroat or "harvest trout," because they return to their spawning streams in September and October. The fish enter streams along the Pacific coast, from northern California to southeastern Alaska.

Unlike steelhead, which spawn in good-sized, fast-flowing coastal streams, sea-run cutthroat are generally found in very small streams that meander gently through meadowlands. They sometimes spawn in the same streams used by coho salmon, but their spawning areas are a little farther upriver.

Once spawning has been completed, usually in February or March, the fish return to the sea. But they do not range as far from the coast as most other anadromous salmonids.

Young cutthroat generally spend two or three years in their spawning streams before smolting and going to sea. Most of the fish are at least 4 years old when they return.

Coastal cutthroat.

Major Cutthroat Subspecies

Cutthroat trout are considered to be a "polytypic" species, meaning that there are many different forms. Where populations of cutthroat trout are geographically isolated, the fish tend to take on unique characteristics. Depending on which authority you choose to believe, there are from 12 to 14 distinct subspecies, some of which are considered to be "threatened," one (West Slope cutthroat) that is

Cutthroat trout range—all subspecies.

a "species of special concern" and one (yellowfin cutthroat) that is extinct.

Today, widespread stocking has mixed the gene pool to the point where subspecies are difficult to recognize in many areas. But purebred subspecies still exist in some waters. The four major subspecies are shown below.

Yellowstone cutthroat (Oncorhynchus clarki bouvieri) have spots above and below the lateral line. The spots are no larger than the pupil of the eye and are more tightly grouped toward the tail.

Lahontan cutthroat (Oncorhynchus clarki henshawi) are the largest cutthroat subspecies. They have widely spaced but fairly uniform spotting. Some of the spots are larger than the pupil.

West Slope cutthroat (Oncorhynchus clarki lewisi) have a spotting pattern similar to that of a Yellowstone, but the spots are smaller. Normally, there are no spots on the front half of the body below the lateral line.

Coastal cutthroat (Oncorhynchus clarki clarki) have silvery sides with heavy spotting. The spots are no larger than the pupil. The slash marks on the throat are usually a faint pink rather than a bright red.

Golden Trout

While every trout species has its admirers, very few would dispute the claim that the golden is the most beautiful of all trout.

Golden trout originated in the Kern River drainage of the Sierra Mountains in central California. In fact, the fish are still called Kern River trout in some areas. The beautiful setting in which the fish were originally found gave rise to their species name, *aguabonita*, meaning pretty water.

The original Kern River stock was exported throughout the inland West and as far away as England before California, for unknown reasons, passed legislation prohibiting the shipping of eggs and fish out of the state.

Goldens are now most common in lakes and streams in mountainous areas of the West. They were originally found only at high altitudes (above 6,000 feet), but they have been stocked at lower elevations where they seem to do equally well.

Some experts theorize that the bright colors of the golden trout evolved to mirror the environment of their native range, the Kern River Basin. There, streambeds consist of red rocks and multi-colored gravels, so the golden's gaudy colors actually serve as camouflage.

Another interesting theory is that severe light, unfiltered by the atmosphere at high elevations, presents deadly levels of solar radiation. The golden's color scheme may actually be a form of protection from that radiation. This theory holds some credence, because the fish lose much of their color intensity when moved to waters at lower elevation.

Golden trout are known for their on-again, off-again feeding habits. Insects and small crustaceans comprise most of their diet. There are times when they will take absolutely nothing other than a fly that precisely imitates their food but, more often, they are much less selective. And there are times when they boil at almost any kind of lure or bait you toss into the water.

This cooperative attitude has led to the fish's demise in most easily-accessible waters. Novelist Stewart Edward White wrote about the vulnerability of the golden trout in his 1904 book, *The Mountains*. In it, he recounted an incident in which a pair of anglers caught 600 goldens in a single day.

Spawning takes place in early to mid-summer when the water temperature reaches about 50°F. A female digs several redds, usually in the tail of a pool in the stream channel or in a tributary.

Golden trout commonly hybridize with rainbows and, on occasion, with cutthroat.

Golden trout range.

These slow-growing fish seldom reach the size of the major stream trout species. Their life span in most waters is about 7 years, and it is rare for them to reach a weight of more than 1 pound in that time. The world-record golden trout, an 11-pounder, was caught in Cook's Lake, Wyoming, in 1948.

The largest golden trout are taken from remote waters at high altitudes (10,000 feet or more). There, the only access is by hiking, and the fish have a better chance of long-term survival.

*Golden trout (*Oncorhynchus aguabonita*) have bright yellow sides with a reddish lateral band that runs through about 10 dark parr marks. Most of the dark spots are above the lateral band, but a few are below it, mainly near the tail. The dorsal, anal and pelvic fins have white tips and the tail is spotted. Spawning males resemble ordinary golden trout, but the colors are even more intense. The lower jaw does not develop a noticeable kype, but becomes slightly longer than normal.*

BULL TROUT

Degradation of stream habitat throughout much of the bull trout's range has placed them on the federal list of "threatened species." Consequently, fishing for them is prohibited until such time populations recover enough to warrant their removal from the list.

Bull trout are one of the lesser known—and lesser appreciated—trout species. These large salmonids have gained a reputation as being serious predators on other trout species. Their fish-eating habits, combined with their reluctance to take a fly, explains their low popularity among some anglers.

Other anglers, however, regard the bull trout as a true trophy. Bulls are extremely tough (but not acrobatic) fighters, waging a stubborn battle in deep water. They sometimes grow to a weight of more than 20 pounds.

Food-habit studies have shown that fish (including trout) do, in fact, make up the bulk of a bull trout's diet. But bulls don't hesitate to take crayfish, clams, snails and immature aquatic insects.

Bull trout have been known to live as long as 20 years. Although they grow slowly in their first few years of life, their growth rate speeds up once they begin to feed on fish. A 10-year-old bull usually weighs about 10 pounds. The world-record bull trout, a 32-pounder, was caught in Lake Pend Orielles, Idaho, in 1949. This fish originally was thought to be a Dolly Varden.

Bull trout are actually char, so they prefer water that is colder than most other trout species prefer, generally in the 45 to 55°F range. Primarily lake-dwellers, bull trout inhabit deep, cold, infertile lakes like those that commonly hold lake trout. But they're also found in large trout streams, usually in the deepest pools.

Not only do bull trout live in the same type of environment as lake trout, they look like lake trout as well. But their spots are usually pink or orange rather than white, and their tail is not as forked.

Bull trout are also easily confused with Dolly Varden. In fact, the two were once considered the same species. This explains why Dollies and bulls often go by the same common names: salmon-trout, red-spotted char and bull char.

The main difference between bull trout and Dolly Varden is that bulls have a much flatter and wider head. Some say that this head shape has evolved to make it easier for them to swallow large fish. Unlike Dollies, bull trout are not anadromous, although there are a few sea-going populations in Alaska.

Bull trout spawn in early fall, but they often begin their upstream migration in late spring or early summer. Both lake- and stream-dwelling

Bull trout range.

bulls require moving water to spawn successfully. They generally build their redds in tributaries of the main river, usually when the water temperature is 45 to 50°F. It's not unusual for bulls to swim more than 50 miles to reach their spawning grounds.

Even if you're not a fan of the bull trout, you can't help but be awestruck by the surroundings in which it is normally found. It inhabits some of the wildest, least-developed and most-beautiful country in the world, including Glacier National Park and the Bob Marshall Wilderness. There, you'll have to share the water only with grizzly bears and bald eagles.

Bull trout (Salvelinus confluentus) *have olive sides with spots that range in color from bright orange to pinkish to whitish. The lower fins have white leading edges. The long, broad, flattened head gives the bull trout a distinctive look. Spawning males develop a bright yellow-orange coloration, the color of the spots intensifies and the lower jaw develops a moderate kype.*

DOLLY VARDEN

These pink-spotted, western char supposedly got their name from a Charles Dickens book, *Barnaby Rudge*, in which one of the characters, Miss Dolly Varden, wore a green dress with pink spots.

Closely related to the bull trout, the Dolly Varden has a much greater propensity toward anadromous behavior. This, along with its considerably narrower head and several other subtle physical differences, convinced biologists that the two were separate species.

Dolly Varden are found mainly along the Pacific Coast, from Washington to Alaska, and around the northern Pacific Rim from Japan to Korea. Dollies are also found in some Siberian waters. Although the majority of the fish are anadromous, land-locked Dollies inhabit many coldwater lakes and streams in the West. Their preferred temperature range is 50 to 55°F.

Dollies are fall spawners, building their redds in the main channel of good-sized streams when the water temperature drops into the low to mid 40s. More than half of the fish die after spawning has been completed.

In most waters, Dollies are considerably smaller than bull trout. A 3-pounder would be a trophy in a mountain stream and anything over 8 pounds would raise eyebrows on a coastal stream.

Surprisingly, Dollies grow fastest in the northern part of

Dolly Varden (Salvelinus malma) can be distinguished from bull trout by their shorter, narrower and less flattened head. The landlocked form (above) has colors that are more intense than those of the sea-run form (below). In small mountain streams, the spotting may lean toward crimson and the body color, dark green. The fins have the distinctive white leading edges found on most chars.

Sea-run Dollies sport a silvery background coloration with pinkish spots. They grow considerably larger than landlocks.

their range. There, a Dolly grows to about 5 pounds in 10 years; in the southern part, they reach only half that size in the same amount of time. The fish are relatively long-lived, surviving up to 19 years. The world-record Dolly, 18 pounds, 9 ounces, was caught in the Mashutuk River, Alaska, in 1993.

The Dolly's habit of eating salmon eggs and sometimes young salmon does little for its popularity among West Coast anglers. But in reality, the fish consume no more eggs than do rainbow or cutthroat. Dolly Varden sometimes feed on insects, and small Dollies can readily be taken on dry flies. Larger ones are more easily caught on spinners, spoons, plugs, streamers or live bait, particularly salmon eggs.

Dolly Varden range.

ARCTIC CHAR

No other freshwater game-fish has a more northerly distribution than the Arctic char. It is found in cold waters of the northern hemisphere, ranging from Alaska and northern Canada to Baffin Island, Greenland, Iceland, northern Norway and northern Siberia.

Landlocked Arctic char are found in the deep, cold, infertile lakes of southern Quebec, southwest Alaska and northern New England, where they are often called "Sunapee" trout. Landlocks are also found in Norway, Sweden, Finland, England, Ireland, Scotland, west-central Europe and Russia.

If you were confused in trying to differentiate bull trout from Dolly Varden, throwing Arctic char into the mix won't help matters. They look almost identical to a Dolly, but the pinkish spots are slightly larger. In Alaska, where both species are common, most anglers don't attempt to distinguish between the two, referring to both species as "char."

Unlike steelhead and salmon, anadromous char seldom range far from the mouth of their home stream. They begin their upstream migration in late summer, spawning in slow-moving pools when the water temperature drops into the low 40s or upper 30s. They overwinter in deep pools or connecting lakes, then return to the sea in spring.

Arctic char (Salvelinus alpinus) are variable in coloration, but landlocks (above) have greenish to grayish sides with large spots that range from reddish to pinkish to off-white. The largest spots are at least the size of the eye's pupil. Like other chars, Arctics have white leading edges on the lower fins.

Landlocked char are found in deep, cold, infertile lakes where they seek out water temperatures in the 45 to 50°F range.

Arctic char are not fussy feeders; they will eat whatever kind of food they can find, including plankton, eels, small fish, crustaceans and insects. Their willingness to take a wide variety of foods explains why they're one of the easiest salmonids to catch. They're easily taken on streamers and will sometimes rise to dry flies, but most anglers rely on flashy spoons.

Although Arctic char grow very slowly, they may live up to 40 years. Sea-run char are formidable fish, reaching

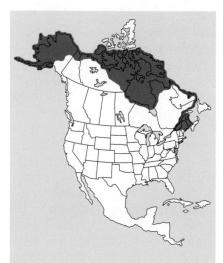

Arctic char range.

weights of 25 pounds and waging a powerful fight when hooked. It's not unusual for one to catapult from the water several times. But the fish lose "steam" after they've been in the stream for a long period.

Landlocked char are considerably smaller than sea-runs, seldom exceeding 8 pounds. The world record Arctic char, weighing 32 pounds, 9 ounces, was taken in the Tree River, Northwest Territories, in 1954.

ARCTIC GRAYLING

Frequently called "the sail-fish of the North," the Arctic grayling has a huge sail-like dorsal fin that is used for maneuvering in the swift current in which it normally lives.

Grayling thrive in cold, clear streams and rivers, but they are also found in the shallow portions of deep, cold, infertile lakes. They prefer icy cold water (42 to 50°F) and a rocky bottom.

The largest grayling populations exist in the Northwest Territories, Alaska, British Columbia, Alberta, Manitoba and Saskatchewan. There are

fishable populations in Montana, Wyoming, Utah and Idaho, mainly in high-elevation lakes.

Although grayling were once common in the Midwest, they were eliminated by fishing pressure and stream-habitat degradation. Efforts are currently being made to reintroduce the fish to some midwestern waters.

Because grayling grow slowly and have a relatively short life span (usually 6 years or less), they seldom reach a weight of more than 4 pounds. In the western states, they rarely exceed 1 pound.

The world-record Arctic grayling, an ounce short of 6 pounds, was taken in the Katseyedie River, Northwest Territories, in 1967.

In early spring, grayling move into small tributary streams to spawn, usually when the water temperature reaches the mid to upper 40s. Unlike other salmonids, they do not dig redds but deposit their eggs on a gravelly or rocky bottom.

In streams, grayling do most of their feeding in shallow riffle areas. In lakes, you'll see them dimpling around inlets and outlets or near downed trees and over-hanging brush along the shoreline.

Grayling prefer small food items such as insects, salmon eggs, crustaceans, clams and snails. This explains why anglers use very small lures, like size 00 to 1 spinners and tiny spoons.

Perhaps the most surface-oriented feeder of all the salmonids, grayling are commonly taken on dry flies in sizes 14 or smaller. When they're not feeding on the surface, they'll readily take small nymphs. Bait fishermen have good success on salmon eggs, worms, maggots, and most other small baits used for stream trout.

Grayling are willing biters, especially when they're feeding in riffles. They can give you a good tussle on light tackle, frequently jumping when first hooked. But they tend to tire quickly.

The ease with which grayling can be caught makes it difficult for fisheries managers to maintain decent populations in easily accessible waters. It's possible, however, if anglers abide by a strict catch-and-release ethic.

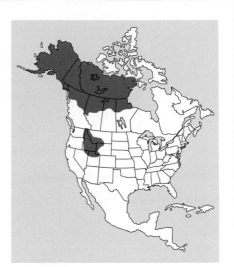

Arctic grayling range.

*The grayling (*Thymallus articus*) has a distinctive dorsal fin with rows of bluish to turquoise spots; its upper margin is often tinged with white or pink. The sides are an iridescent purplish-gray, with scales much larger than those of other salmonids. The tail, pectoral and anal fins are usually yellowish and the pelvic fins have lengthwise stripes of black and pink. The male (above) has a long dorsal fin which, when folded down, extends almost to the adipose fin.*

The female grayling has a much shorter dorsal fin than that of the male. When folded down, it falls well short of the adipose fin.

THE WATERS

All successful stream trout anglers have one skill in common: The ability to quickly recognize productive trout water.

Trout: Stream-Fishing Strategies

TROUT HABITAT

Stream-fishing for trout is one of the most challenging—and addictive—forms of angling. And it's easy to understand why. Every trout stream is unique, so you must learn the idiosyncrasies of each stream you fish. But there's even more to it than that. Nature has a way of frequently rearranging stream habitat, so the learning process is continuous.

Trout can survive in a wide variety of flowing water, ranging from ice-cold mountain brooks fed by melting snow to farm-country streams the color of heavily-creamed coffee. But regardless of outward appearances, every stream must meet certain physical and chemical requirements in order to provide permanent habitat for trout.

WATER TEMPERATURE

Trout require a year-round supply of relatively cold water. Unless a stream is located in the Far North, or at a very high altitude, it must be fed by spring water, snowmelt, runoff from a glacier or water drawn from the bottom of a deep reservoir in order to remain cold enough for trout throughout the year.

The temperature preferences of trout species vary widely, as the chart at the right shows. Very few streams have water cold enough to support chars or grayling, which generally require water in the mid-50s or below. But other trout are comfortable at water temperatures in the low to mid 60s and some, such as rainbows and browns, can tolerate temperatures

Preferred Water Temperatures

Species	Preferred Temperature Range
Chars	
Brook trout	52-56°F
Bull trout	45-55
Dolly Varden	50-55
Arctic char	45-50
Other Salmonids	
Brown trout	60-65
Rainbow trout	55-60
Cutthroat trout	55-62
Golden trout	57-62
Grayling	42-50

Sources of Cold Water

Underground springs are the main source of cold water in the majority of trout streams.

Meltwater from snow-capped peaks and glaciers is the source of cold water in many mountain streams and even in some streams at lower elevations.

approaching 80 for short periods of time.

Many streams have water cold enough for trout for 9 or 10 months out of the year. In midsummer, however, elevated water temperatures place trout under stress and may, in fact, kill them. In years past, many such streams were managed for trout on a put-and-take basis, but that type of management is seldom done today.

In most streams, the water temperature increases along the length of the stream course. If a stream originates from a large spring, for instance, the headwaters area may be cold enough for brook trout. But as the water flows over the ground, it gradually warms up and becomes more suitable for browns and rainbows. And toward the lower end of the stream, conditions may be better suited to smallmouth bass and catfish.

In some streams, the coldest water is well downstream of the headwaters. This would happen, for example, if a major coldwater tributary or spring entered the stream midway through its course.

Although the temperature of a stream depends primarily on the source of water, there are other contributing factors including the *gradient*, or slope, of the streambed, the shape of the streambed and the amount of shade along the stream course.

GRADIENT

The reason the gradient of a stream affects water temperature is simple: the flatter the streambed, the slower the water moves and the more heat it absorbs from the sun. Even if a stream has water cold enough for brook trout, the water will not stay cold if beavers dam the stream and turn it into a series of flat pools.

Gradient affects the quality of a trout stream in other ways as well. A stream with a moderate gradient (below) is ideal, because the current speed is just right to create the diverse pool-riffle-run habitat (p. 56) that fulfills all of a trout's needs.

If the gradient is too high, a stream usually lacks good-sized pools, so trout have to take cover in small pockets behind rocks and other obstructions. Such streams usually have a poor food supply as well.

If the gradient is too low, the current is slow and silt tends to accumulate on the bottom. This clogs up the gravel, reducing insect production and suffocating trout eggs.

SHAPE OF STREAMBED

The quality of a trout stream depends, in part, on the cross-sectional and longitudinal shape of its streambed.

As a rule, a good trout stream has a deep, narrow streambed rather than a shallow, wide one.

The Importance of Gradient

High-gradient streams may drop as much as 300 feet per mile. The bottom consists of large rocks and boulders, and there are few holding areas for trout.

Low-gradient streams—those that drop less than 30 feet per mile—are usually too warm for trout and their silty bottom is not conducive to food production or trout spawning.

Moderate-gradient streams are best-suited to trout because they have a variety of habitat types ranging from deep, slow-moving, sandy-bottomed pools to swift, rocky runs and riffles.

The Importance of Streambed Shape

A wide, shallow streambed is not well-suited to trout because it tends to have warm water, slow current and a silty bottom.

A deep, narrow streambed keeps the water temperature cool and the current fast enough to prevent siltation of the bottom.

A meandering streambed features pools, flats, riffles, rapids, runs, bars, eddies, undercut banks and other habitat types that provide the feeding, resting and spawning sites that trout require.

A channelized stream has a uniform width, depth and current pattern. Cover is generally lacking and food is in short supply.

In a wide streambed, a larger percentage of the water is exposed to the air and the warming rays of the sun, so the water tends to warm faster than it would in a narrow, deep bed.

One of the best ways to improve a trout stream is to narrow its channel. Natural resources agencies in many states conduct habitat-improvement projects intend-ed primarily to reduce the width of streams that have been widened by floods or beaver activity.

In its natural state, a stream tends to meander across its floodplain in snakelike fashion, resulting in a diverse streambed with the characteristic pool-riffle-run configuration.

When a stream is channel-ized (artificially straightened), however, habitat diversity decreases and the trout population declines or disappears.

Straightening the channel results in loss of total stream mileage as well. A meander-ing stream that measured two miles in length, for example, may cover only one mile after all the bends have been removed.

Understanding the Pool-Riffle-Run Sequence

Because of the powerful excavating force of moving water, a natural, unaltered stream consists of a recurring sequence of three distinct types of habitat: pools, riffles and runs. Each of these habitats is characterized by the following:

Pools
- Slow current.
- A relatively smooth surface.
- Fine bottom materials such as silt, sand or small gravel.

Riffles
- Moderate to fast current.
- A turbulent surface.
- Less than 2 feet deep.
- Coarse bottom materials such as boulders, rubble or large gravel.

Runs
- More than 2 feet deep.
- Slightly slower and less turbulent than riffles.
- Coarse bottom materials such as boulders, rubble or large gravel.

Pools provide an ideal resting area and a deepwater retreat for the stream's largest trout. Many trout build their redds in the tails of pools, where the rising bottom keeps water flowing through the gravel and aerating the eggs.

Riffles produce an abundance of aquatic insects and are important morning and evening feeding areas. Trout may stay in riffle areas all day if there are good-sized boulders to provide slackwater resting areas.

Runs are prime feeding areas because trout can lie along the edge of the swift current and dart out to grab drifting food. And runs are deep enough that trout can feed without fear of attack by predatory birds, such as kingfishers and herons.

The pool-riffle-run sequence is much more apparent in some streams than in others. It is easy to distinguish in a small stream of moderate gradient. But in a large, slow-moving stream, these habitat types tend to blend together. Savvy anglers take time to become familiar with the pool-riffle-run sequence in waters they commonly fish, because they know it is the key to finding trout.

The fast water in a (1) riffle digs out a deeper channel, called a (2) run, just downstream. As the water in the run deepens, the current speed slows, forming a (3) pool. Because of the slower current, sediment settles out at the downstream end of the pool, constricting the flow, speeding up the current and forming another riffle. This sequence repeats itself approximately once for every seven stream widths. If a stream averages 10 feet wide, for example, a new pool-riffle-run sequence occurs about every 70 feet.

Trout: Stream-Fishing Strategies

The Importance of Shade

Too much shade prevents sunlight from reaching the streambed. Production of aquatic foods is minimal and trout growth is slow.

An unshaded stream heats up quickly; it may support trout in its upper reaches and around springs, but the lower reaches are generally too warm.

SHADE

Shade is generally beneficial to a trout stream, because it prevents the sun from warming the water too much. Shade is most commonly furnished by trees and bushes along the streambank but, in some narrow streams, overhanging grasses and sedges provide the necessary shade. All these plants help stabilize the bank, preventing erosion and widening of the stream channel.

Overgrazing by cattle is often the reason for a lack of shade. The animals graze right up to the streambank, preventing growth of trees, bushes and tall grasses. In this situation, the best solution is to fence out the cattle.

But too much shade can be a problem as well. For good food production, some sunlight must reach the stream bottom to fuel the aquatic food chain. Fisheries managers have discovered that production of aquatic insects improves greatly on heavily-shaded streams when trees and streamside brush are thinned out or removed. This, in turn, improves the growth rate of trout.

In any habitat-improvement project, the idea is to achieve the right balance of shade to keep the water warm enough for good food production yet cool enough for long-term survival of trout.

WATER FERTILITY

Trout can survive in streams of most any fertility level, but the best trout streams have the dissolved nutrients necessary to provide a good supply of food.

Trout streams are sometimes categorized according to their fertility level. Limestone streams, the most fertile type, are fed by underground springs that bubble up from limestone aquifers. The springs are rich in minerals (mainly calcium carbonate), explaining why these streams produce so much plant and invertebrate life and such abundant fish crops.

Freestone streams, on the other hand, are fed by snowmelt or surface runoff and have a very low mineral content. In fact, some say that the term "freestone" means free of limestone. Freestone streams generally have smaller trout crops and the fish grow more slowly.

TYPES OF TROUT STREAMS

Scientists who study streams have come up with numerous classification schemes. Depending on which expert you choose to believe, streams can be grouped according to fertility, gradient, temperature, age, fish-species suitability or some combination of the above. Unfortunately, none of these classification methods is very helpful when it comes to trout streams.

The majority of trout streams, however, are classi- fied by trout anglers as lime- stone or freestone. The most important types of limestone and freestone streams are shown on these pages. Other common types of trout streams are depicted on pages 60-61.

Types of Limestone Streams

Spring creeks are fed by large under- ground springs. They generally have very clear water, lush vegeta- tion, an abun- dance of insect life, plenty of crus- taceans and a large crop of fast- growing trout.

Streams flowing over limestone bedrock pick up minerals from the streambed. Although not as clear or heavily vegetated as spring creeks, these streams have an abundance of food and an excellent trout population.

Mountain streams, usually fed by meltwater from snowpack or glaciers, have fast current and cold, infertile water with a poor supply of food and a relatively sparse crop of slow-growing trout.

Foothill streams can be good trout producers, even though their water is not particularly high in fertility. Many such streams are fed by a combination of snowmelt, surface runoff and springflow. They normally have a medium gradient and a rocky streambed with the typical pool-riffle-run configuration.

Tailwater streams are fed by cold water drawn off the bottom of a deep reservoir. Because the water temperature changes very little throughout the year, these streams produce an abundance of food and large crops of fast-growing trout. Stream levels may fluctuate tremendously throughout the day, however, as water is released to drive power-generating turbines.

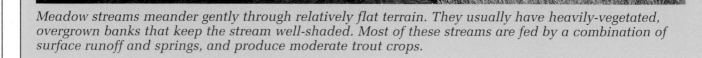

Meadow streams meander gently through relatively flat terrain. They usually have heavily-vegetated, overgrown banks that keep the stream well-shaded. Most of these streams are fed by a combination of surface runoff and springs, and produce moderate trout crops.

Coastal streams draw seasonal runs of anadromous trout and salmon. Some such streams hold fish nearly year-round, as migratory trout enter the stream in fall and winter to spawn in the spring. Most coastal streams also have resident trout populations.

Large-lake tributaries, such as streams flowing into the Great Lakes, also have seasonal trout runs. Rainbows enter the streams to spawn in spring and sometimes return in fall for a "mock" spawning run. Brown and brook trout move into the streams only in fall. Many such streams also have populations of resident trout.

How to "Read" the Water

An accomplished stream-trout angler spends a good deal of time walking the bank to study current patterns and bottom contours in an attempt to determine the best trout holding spots, or "lies." This streamside research, called "reading the water," is just as important as how you present your lure or bait.

When doing your streamside reconnaissance, try to find a high overlook that enables you to see down into the water. Always wear polarized sunglasses and try to keep the sun at your back to minimize glare. It's easiest to see into the water when the sun is high.

In many cases you won't be able to see what's beneath the water's surface but, if you understand how the force of moving water shapes the stream channel, you'll have a pretty good idea of the trout-holding potential of a given spot.

For example, if you see current deflecting off a point on one side of the stream and disappearing under the bank on the other side, you know the bank is undercut and, in all likelihood, the undercut holds trout.

Reading the water also involves looking for boulders, logs and other objects that break the current and create slack-water shelter for trout. In clear water, you may be able to see these objects, but there will be times when their presence is known only by the current patterns they create.

When you see a large "standing wave" in a swift run, for instance, you know there is a good-sized boulder beneath the surface deflecting the current upward. You also know that the boulder is creating a trout-holding eddy on the downstream side (p. 64).

Sometimes the color of the water is a clue to finding trout. Most anglers know that a deep pool looks darker than the surrounding water on a sunny day, but subtle coloration differences can be important too. A slightly darker seam through the middle of a run, for instance, may be only a few inches deeper than the water on either side, but trout hold there because the current is a little slower.

It's also important for stream-trout anglers to have a basic understanding of man-made stream-improvement structures. Devices such as crib shelters (p. 65) are often constructed on degraded streams. The undercut they provide may reach up to 6 feet under the bank and hold dozens of trout.

Because these structures are designed to look natural, anglers may not even know they are present unless they know exactly what to look for.

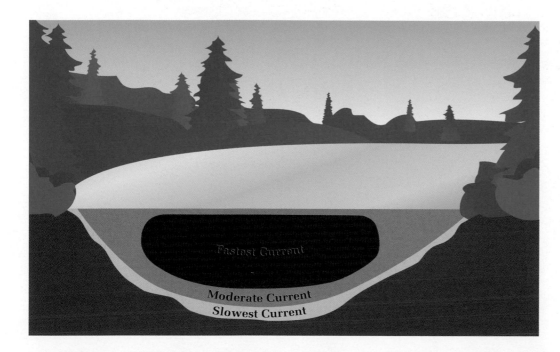

Fastest Current

Moderate Current

Slowest Current

Friction with the stream bottom and sides, as well as the air, causes the current speed to vary over the stream's cross-section. In a symmetrical stream channel, the fastest current (deep purple) is in the middle and the slowest (pink) in a narrow band along the bottom. The remainder of the stream has moderate current (purple). Along a bend, the zone of fastest water shifts to the outside of the channel.

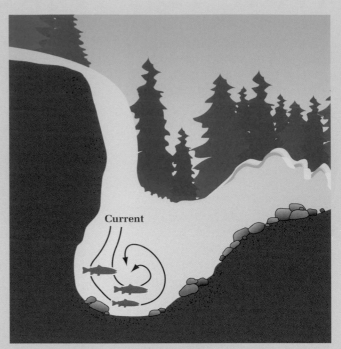

Water tumbling over a falls excavates a "plunge pool" at the base; this pool may be deeper than the falls is high. A large eddy forms at the base of the falls, creating an undercut that may hold some of the stream's largest trout.

A standing wave forms in fast water when a boulder deflects the water upward. The eddy that forms downstream of the boulder is often a good trout lie.

In a meandering stream, look for trout (1) beneath undercuts that form along outside bends and (2) below point bars that form on inside bends. These features are seldom present in streams with a straight channel.

Current flowing cross-stream and disappearing under the bank reveals an undercut. Some under- cuts extend several feet under the bank, providing the stream's best trout cover.

Deep pools usually have a dark bluish-green or even a black color. Deep pools with boulders or logs for cover usually hold the stream's largest trout.

A deep slot appears as a darker channel within a run. Trout are likely to hold in the deepest part of the slot, where the current is lightest.

Eddies often form on both the upstream and downstream side of boulders and other large objects. A boil, formed by water deflecting upward, forms just downstream of the object, pinpointing its location.

Current seams identify the margin between slow and fast water. Trout often hold along the slow side of a current seam and then dart out into the fast water to grab drifting food.

Crib shelters are constructed by burying horizontal pilings to create a deep undercut. A deflector on the opposite side of the stream directs water toward the crib, eroding the bank beneath it.

THE GEAR

*B*ecause of the wary nature of stream trout, anglers must be extra choosy in the equipment they select.

Trout: Stream-Fishing Strategies

RODS & REELS

The mere mention of stream-fishing for trout conjures up the image of a fly fisher gracefully laying out a perfect loop of line with a fly rod. But stream-trout fishermen use many other kinds of tackle as well, ranging from ultralight spinning gear to beefy baitcasting outfits.

FLY RODS

For some, the choice of a fly rod depends more on tradition than functionality. There is a certain satisfaction in using a handcrafted bamboo rod that took an accomplished rodmaker hundreds of hours to construct. But there is no arguing the fact that today's space-age graphite fly rods far outperform those bamboo masterpieces.

If you're more interested in performance than tradition, here are the main considerations in choosing a fly rod:

• **Material**. Choose a quality graphite rod with a high modulus (stiffness-to-weight ratio). The extra stiffness makes it easier to pick up line off the water and gives you more power to propel it, enabling you to make longer, more effortless casts. Very few anglers now use fiberglass or bamboo rods because they lack this stiffness.

• **Weight**. The weight designation of a fly rod specifies the line weight for which the rod is intended. A 5-weight fly rod, for example, should be used with a 5-weight line, but it may also handle a 4-weight or 6-weight line.

Fly rods come in weights ranging from 1 to 15, but most stream-trout anglers use rods in the 3- to 7-weight range. If you're fishing steelhead or other exceptionally large trout, however, you'll probably need a 9- or 10-weight rod.

• **Action**. Although some manufacturers designate the action of their fly rods, most do not. But action (where the rod bends) is important because it greatly affects casting performance.

Most fly fishers prefer a fast-action rod because of its superior casting performance, but a medium- or slow-action is a better choice when fishing a dry fly with a very light tippet. A slower rod is more forgiving, reducing the chances of snapping your tippet on the hookset.

• **Length**. The current trend in fly fishing is toward longer rods, because they enable you to handle more line. In the past, long rods simply were not practical because they were too heavy. But with the advent of high-modulus graphite, you can get more length for the weight, so some anglers are now using 9½- or even 10-foot rods.

Yet longer rods are not always better. When you're fishing in tight quarters—such as a narrow, brushy stream—a rod in the 6- to 7-foot range is a better choice.

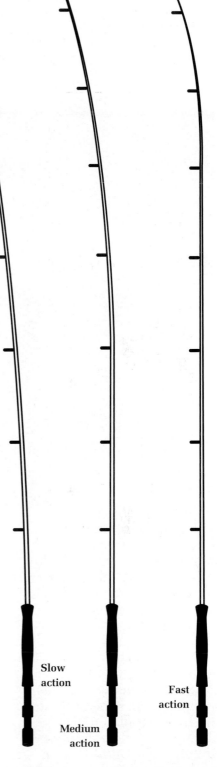

Slow action

Medium action

Fast action

Rod actions. *A slow-action rod bends over most of its length, a medium-action rod starts bending slightly before the midpoint and a fast-action rod bends only in the last one-third of its length.*

FLY REELS

The standard wisdom in selecting a fly reel for stream-trout fishing is that almost any reel will do. While that's true most of the time, you may wish you had spent a few extra bucks when you hook a big trout and it starts smoking line off your reel. Here's what to look for in a fly reel:

•**Size/Capacity**. Your reel must be large enough to hold the line you plan to use, along with at least 150 yards of 20- to 30-pound Dacron backing. For steelhead and other large, powerful trout, allow for at least 200 yards of backing.

•**Type of Action**. When referring to a fly reel, the term "action" means the rate at which the reel picks up line. A single-action reel, for example, has a gear ratio of 1:1, meaning that the spool turns once for every turn of the reel handle. A multiplying reel has a gear ratio of 1.5:1 to 3:1, meaning that the spool turns from 1.5 to 3 times for every turn of the reel handle. Multipliers, therefore, have a much faster retrieve, making it possible to take up slack in a hurry should a big fish change direction and run toward you.

•**Type of Drive**. The majority of fly reels sold today are direct-drive, which means that the reel handle turns along with the spool. Direct-drive reels are adequate for most stream-trout fishing but, should a large trout make a power run, the handle rapidly spins backward. If you happen to touch it, the line could snap or you could skin your knuckles. Anti-reverse reels, on the other hand, have a clutch mechanism that prevents the handle from spinning backward.

•**Material**. Most modern fly reels are made of aluminum or graphite. These lightweight materials are ideal for matching up with today's feather-light rods. The best reels are machined from a block of aluminum alloy, so they have very fine tolerances and an extremely smooth action. But they may cost $500 or more, many times the price of a stamped aluminum or graphite reel.

A cheap fly reel has sloppy tolerances, so the leader can easily slip behind the spool. This won't happen on a machined aluminum reel.

30 feet in length. And a long rod is simply not practical on a narrow, brushy stream; there, a fisherman would do better with a 5-foot rod.

•**Power**. An ultralight to light spinning rod with 2- to 4-pound mono is ideal for tossing lures weighing $\frac{1}{32}$ to $\frac{1}{4}$ ounce and catching trout weighing up to 2 pounds.

You'll need a medium-power rod with 6- to 8-pound mono to handle heavier lures ($\frac{1}{4}$ to $\frac{5}{8}$ ounce) and land larger trout.

•**Action**. For casting very light lures, you need a slow-action spinning rod that flexes over most of its length. If your rod is too stiff, it will not flex, or *load*, so you will have to "throw" the lure rather than letting the rod do the work. A medium-action rod (one that starts bending in the middle) is the best all-around choice; it allows you to cast most trout lures and gives you a strong hookset.

A slow-action rod is best for casting tiny spinning lures because it loads well on the backcast.

SPINNING RODS

A spinning outfit makes it possible to toss small spinners, spoons and other light "hardware" that would be impossible to cast with bait-casting gear. You can even spinfish with a fly, if you attach a plastic casting bubble (p. 139) for weight.

When selecting a spinning rod, consider the following:

•**Material**. The best spinning rods are made of the same material as the best fly rods—high-modulus graphite.

Not only does a high-modulus rod give you excellent casting performance, its light weight allows you to cast with less effort.

•**Length.** The trend in spinning, as in flycasting, is toward longer rods, which enable longer casts. On large western streams, anglers use spinning rods up to 9 feet long for tossing hardware to the opposite bank. But in most trout streams, long casts are unnecessary; the average cast will be less than

SPINNING REELS

You don't need an expensive spinning reel to catch stream trout, but you should consider the following when making your purchase:

• **Size**. Your spinning reel should balance well with the rod you are using; otherwise, casting will be a lot more work. As a rule, you'll need a reel weighing about 7 or 8 ounces to balance with an ultralight rod. A 10- or 11-ounce reel is a better choice for a medium-power rod.

Line capacity is not much of an issue in most stream-trout fishing. But you may need a high-capacity reel on large western trout streams where you're making long casts for large trout.

• **Drag**. When you're fishing for small- to medium-sized trout, the type of drag is not too important. But when you hook a big trout, the last thing you want is a sticky drag. As a rule, a front drag is much smoother and more reliable than a rear drag. Like disk brakes, the washers on a front drag exert pressure on a large, flat surface.

• **Shape of Spool**. For best casting perfor-

Make sure your reel is well-matched to your rod by balancing it on your finger as shown. The balance point should be just ahead of the front of the reel.

mance, choose a reel with a wide spool. If the spool is too narrow, the line comes off in tight coils, creating friction on the line guides and shortening casting distance. Another drawback to a narrow spool: You'll have to respool more often to keep the line level near the spool's lip. Otherwise, casting perfor-

mance will suffer when you lose even a little line.

BAITCASTING RODS

Used primarily for steelhead and other large trout, baitcasting gear is the best choice for casting with heavy monofilament. On a spinning outfit, heavy mono tends to

A steelhead rod has the length and stiffness necessary to turn a powerful fish in fast current.

come off the spool in coils, but on a baitcaster, the rotating spool keeps the line relatively straight. Here are the main concerns in selecting a baitcasting rod:

•**Length**. Most "steelhead" rods are 8 to 10 feet in length, so they cast well and enable you to control a powerful fish in swift water, directing it where you want it to go.

•**Power**. For casting lures weighing up to 2 ounces or drift-fishing with a heavy sinker (p. 110), you'll need a medium-heavy or heavy power rod.

•**Action**. Steelhead rods usually have a fast or extra-fast action for maximum sensitivity and hook-setting speed.

•**Handle**. An extra-long handle is a must. It enables you to make two-handed casts for maximum distance and, by holding the butt against your forearm, you have more leverage to control a hooked fish.

BAITCASTING REELS

You'll need a sturdy baitcasting reel to withstand the abuse from casting heavy baits and tangling with trout that could weigh ten pounds or more. A good baitcasting reel should have the following features:

•**Capacity**. Your reel should hold a minimum of 200 yards of 14-pound-test mono. A large capacity spool not

Advantages of a Long-Handled Rod

By using your free hand on the lower part of the butt to generate more rod speed, you can greatly increase casting distance.

To exert extra pressure on a large trout, keep the butt of the rod tucked up against your forearm, as shown.

only allows longer casts, it prevents break-offs should a big fish make a long run.

•**Drag**. Most quality baitcasting reels have a reliable star drag, but on cheaper models the drag tends to be jerky. If the drag happens to stick when a big fish makes a run, the line will break instantly. The first thing you should do after purchasing a baitcasting reel is test the

drag; if it's not smooth, return the reel.

•**Level-wind**. The level-wind mechanism should travel back and forth across the spool when you cast, not stay in one place. With a stationary level-wind, the line runs through the guide at too much of an angle, creating extra friction and reducing casting distance.

Baitcasting reels used for large trout generally have a strong metal frame and weigh 12 to 14 ounces.

LINE

No matter if you prefer fly-casting, spinning or baitcasting gear, your choice of line is of utmost importance. With the wrong line, you won't be able to present your fly, bait or lure properly.

FLY LINE

Fly line serves a much different function than other types of lines. In fly fishing, you are actually casting the line which, in turn, propels the nearly weightless fly.

Fly lines come in a wide variety of weights, tapers and buoyancies; your choice depends on the type and size of your fly, how far you want to cast it and how deep you want to fish it. Here are some tips for making the right selection:

• **Weight**. As discussed earlier, your fly line's weight must match your rod's weight. Otherwise you will not be able to cast as well as you should. Although fly lines are available in weights ranging from 1 (the lightest) to 15 (the heaviest), most stream-trout fishermen use lines in the 3- to 7-weight range.

Fly-line weight affects casting performance and determines what size fly you can cast. A 3-weight rod, for example, works best for casting flies in sizes 12 to 28; a 7-weight, sizes 4 to 16. A light line simply does not have the punch necessary to propel a heavy or wind-resistant fly.

•**Buoyancy**. You must choose a line with a buoyancy suited to the type of fly you're using and the desired fishing depth. There are three popular types.

Floating lines, abbreviated as F, are by far the most widely used. Impregnated with air bubbles, these lines float high on the surface, so they work especially well with dry flies. But they can also be used for shallow presentations with subsurface flies.

Sinking lines (S) are designed for fishing subsurface flies at depths as great as 20 feet. These lines sink at varying rates, depending on the amount of lead or tungsten particles in the coating. Sinking lines are much more difficult to cast than floating lines.

Floating/Sinking lines (FS), also called sink-tip lines, have a 5- to 25-foot sinking tip section; the remainder of the line floats. These lines are much easier to cast

than full-sinking lines, but they will not fish as deep.

•**Taper**. The way a fly line is tapered affects casting performance and delicacy of your presentation. There are four main types of tapers.

Double-taper lines, abbreviated as DT, are tapered on both ends. They work well for short- to medium-distance casting and, because the end of the line is relatively thin, it alights delicately. When one end of the line wears out, reverse the line.

Weight-forward lines (WF) have a thick, heavy front end. They are a good choice for making long casts and punching into the wind, but they lack the delicacy of a double-taper.

Shooting-taper lines (ST), also called shooting-head lines, are the best choice for making very long casts. The short, heavy head propels the the thinner running line, enabling you to cast more than 100 feet. But these lines splash down even harder than weight-forwards and are prone to tangling.

Level lines (L), are the same

diameter over their length. They are the least expensive type of fly line, but their inferior casting performance limits their popularity.

SPINNING & BAITCASTING LINES

Because trout are known to be quite "line-shy," most anglers who use spinning or baitcasting gear rely on clear mono or mono tinted the same color as the water.

Extra-limp mono is the best choice for casting the light lures normally used in stream-trout fishing. But a hard-finish, abrasion-resistant line is a better choice for drift-fishing or casting in a rocky stream where constant scuffing of your line is a problem.

Superline, nylon or Dacron line, fluorescent mono or any high-visibility mono is seldom used in stream-trout fishing.

Understanding Taper

(1) Double-taper lines are tapered equally on both ends, (2) weight-forward lines have a thick belly behind the front taper, (3) shooting-taper lines have a short, compact head followed by a long monofilament or coated-Dacron running line, (4) level lines have the same diameter over their entire length.

For best casting performance, the diameter of your tippet must suit the size of your fly. Some anglers use a micrometer to make sure their tippet is the right diameter.

FLY LEADERS

The leader is a crucial part of any fly-fishing outfit, but it is the component that most anglers give the least thought. Without the right leader you can make a beautiful cast—with the line rolling over gracefully—but the leader will not follow. It will tumble to the water in a pile, causing your cast to fall short of its mark and possibly spooking the fish.

For the energy of the cast to transfer smoothly from the line to the leader, the leader must be tapered. Fly anglers use two kinds of tapered leaders: knotted and knotless.

Knotted leaders consist of several sections of different diameter mono, tied together with blood knots (opposite). One advantage to a knotted leader is that you can modify it to suit the fishing situation. And when the tippet (end

section) becomes frayed or shortened too much, you can simply cut it off and replace it with a fresh line section.

Knotless leaders consist of a single piece of factory-tapered mono. They turn over easily and, because there are no knots, they don't collect bits of weed and debris.

Another consideration in leader selection is the diameter of the tippet, which is measured on the traditional "X" scale. The higher the X number, the smaller the tippet diameter (remember that the X number is not the same as pound test). As a rule, the smaller the fly, the smaller diameter tippet you'll need for good casting (chart, opposite). And a light tippet is harder for trout to see.

The length of your leader is also important. In dry-fly fishing, for example, you need a long leader, usually

from 8 to 12 feet, to minimize spooking. But a subsurface fly and sinking line call for a short leader, sometimes only 3 or 4 feet in length, to help the fly sink with the line.

Although most fly leaders are made of ordinary nylon monofilament, braided-mono leaders are also available. Some anglers prefer the braided type because they cast well and offer a little more cushion when you set the hook.

Fluorocarbon leader material is rapidly gaining popularity because it is nearly invisible in water. It is also more abrasion-resistant than nylon and less affected by sunlight. But it is much more expensive, its knot strength is inferior and, because it has only half the stretch of nylon, tends to break more frequently on the hookset.

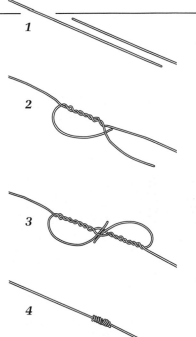

Make a knotted leader by joining sections of mono with blood knots. To tie a blood knot, (1) hold the lines alongside each other, with the ends facing opposite directions; (2) wrap one line around the other 4-5 times, and pass the free end between the two lines, as shown; (3) repeat step 2 with the other line; (4) pull on both lines to snug up the knot.

Tippet Diameter vs. Fly Size

X–Number	Strength* (# test)	Diameter	Fly Size
8X	1.0-1.8	.003"	20-28
7X	1.1-2.5	.004"	18-26
6X	1.4-3.5	.005"	14-22
5X	2.4-4.8	.006"	10-18
4X	3.1-6.0	.007"	8-16
3X	3.8-8.5	.008"	6-14
2X	4.5-11.5	.009"	4-10
1X	5.5-13.5	.010"	1/0-6
0X	6.5-15.5	.011"	3/0-2

*Strength of tippet materials of the same diameter varies greatly, depending on the manufacturer.

How to Construct a Fly Leader

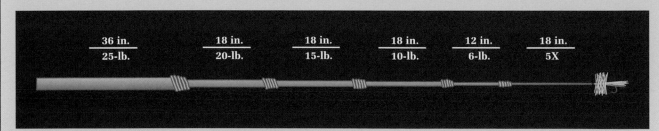

A fly leader consists of a butt section (about 60 percent of the leader's total length), a midsection (20 percent) and a tippet (20 percent). Each of these sections may include more than one piece of mono to create the desired taper.

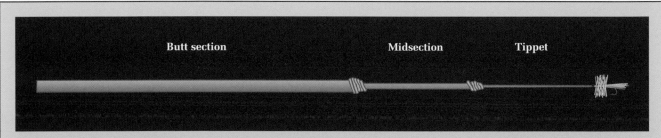

A typical leader for medium-duty trout fishing with a 5- to 7-weight outfit includes a butt section made of 25-, 20- and 15-pound mono; a midsection of 10- and 6-pound mono and a 5X tippet.

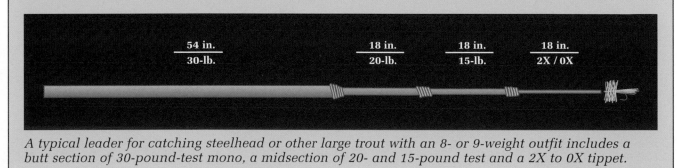

A typical leader for catching steelhead or other large trout with an 8- or 9-weight outfit includes a butt section of 30-pound-test mono, a midsection of 20- and 15-pound test and a 2X to 0X tippet.

WADERS & HIP BOOTS

Wading gear is to a stream fishermen what a boat and motor is to a lake fisherman. Without good wading gear, a stream-trout angler would not be able to put a lure into many of the stream's most productive spots.

There are two popular types of wading gear: chest waders and hip boots. If the water in which you're wading is less than thigh-high, you can get by with hip boots; otherwise, you'll need chest waders. In hot weather, many anglers prefer to wear shorts or quick-drying pants along with wading sandals.

When purchasing wading gear, you'll have to decide on the best material, style and type of

sole for the conditions in which you'll be fishing.

MATERIALS

In years past, practically all wading gear was made of rubber. Although rubber gear is still available, modern fabrics are superior in most respects. The most commonly used materials include:

• **Nylon**. This is the lightest material used for making wading gear and is quite economical. Nylon gear has no insulation, so it is used mainly in warm weather.

• **Neoprene**. Because neoprene flexes when you move, wading gear made of this material is quite comfortable. Neoprene is warm and surprisingly durable and, should you trip and fall into the

Chest waders.

water, it will help keep you afloat. But neoprene wading gear is expensive and

Hip Boots.

usually too warm for fishing in hot weather.

• **Breathable fabrics**. Gore-Tex and other breathable fabrics make the most comfortable wading gear. They weigh no more than nylon, but they are much cooler because air can pass through them.

• **Rubber**. Although rubber wading gear is durable and inexpensive, it is very heavy and is not a good choice for fishing in either hot or cold weather.

STYLE

Both waders and hip boots come in two basic styles: boot-foot and stocking-foot. Here are the advantages and disadvantages:

• **Boot-foot**. This style fits more loosely than the stocking-foot style, so it is easier to slip on and pull off. And in cold weather, it won't restrict your circulation, so your feet will stay warmer.

• **Stocking-foot**. This type of wading gear has a separate wading boot, so you get more ankle support than you do with boot-foot gear.

Wading Gear Styles

Boot-foot wading gear should fit tightly around the ankles so it doesn't pull off in sticky mud.

Stocking foot wading gear is usually worn with ankle guards to keep gravel out of the boots.

SOLE TYPE

To get good traction and avoid slipping and going for a swim, your wading gear must have the right kind of sole. Here are the most popular types:

• **Felt soles**. Felt is a good all-around choice for different bottom types. It gives you good traction even on mossy rocks. Although felt soles wear out quickly, you can replace them by gluing on new ones.

• **Studded soles**. Metal studs add traction to felt soles, giving you the best possible footing for fishing on slippery rocks or in swift current.

• **Lug soles**. These common soles are adequate for a sandy or muddy bottom, but they have poor traction on slippery rocks or in fast water.

Wading Gear Soles

Felt soles come with some wading gear, but you can also purchase them separately and glue them on.

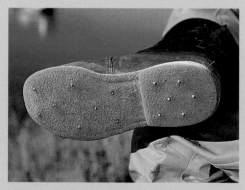

Metal studs give felt soles extra traction and increase the sole's life.

Lug soles feature molded-rubber cleats that are durable but provide relatively poor traction.

BOATS & MOTORS

A boat is not necessary for the majority of stream-trout fishing, but when you're chasing trout on a big river it opens up a lot of options.

Some of the prime mid-river pools, for example, may be inaccessible to wading anglers because the water is simply too deep or too swift. And deep pools along a high bank are much easier to fish from a boat than from shore.

A boat also enables you to cover a lot more water than you can by wading. You can easily float more than 10 miles in a day, working all of the very best water in that reach.

You can use practically any type of shallow-draft boat—including canoes, jon boats and small aluminum semi-Vs—for fishing in a good-sized trout stream. But serious big-river fishermen rely on specialty boats designed for specific purposes.

McKenzie River boats, for example, have swept-up ends and a widely flared middle, making them surprisingly easy to maneuver with a pair of long oars. They are quite stable and draw very little water. McKenzie boats are often made to accommodate a small outboard motor.

Some anglers prefer inflatable rafts to McKenzie boats, because inflatables can be carried to the water almost anywhere along the stream course. But they are much less comfortable and not nearly as easy to maneuver as a McKenzie boat. Many rafts can also accommodate an outboard.

Jet boats make it possible to speed over shallow flats and riffles only a few inches deep. Such water would be impossible to cross with an ordinary outboard. The downside to a jet drive is that it has about one-third less power than a prop-driven motor of the same size.

McKenzie River boats are stable enough that the angler in the bow can safely stand while casting. Knee braces in the bow provide the necessary support. Most McKenzie boats are made of wood or fiberglass, so they are sturdy and quiet.

Inflatable rafts, made of highly durable, puncture-resistant fabric, offer the ultimate in portability. Rafts in the 12- to 16-foot range are most commonly used for stream-trout fishing.

Jet boats have a flat-bottomed hull, usually made of heavy-gauge aluminum, and are powered by an outboard or inboard jet-drive motor. Jet drives propel the boat by sucking in water and jetting it out, much like an aircraft engine uses air for propulsion.

ACCESSORIES

When you see a stream-trout fisherman decked out in a fancy fishing vest, pockets bulging with tools and gadgets, you might get the impression that it's all for looks. But when you're fishing a trout stream, you have to be self-contained, no matter if you're a fly fisherman or a spin-fisherman. Otherwise you'll be hiking back to your vehicle every time you need to re-rig.

Here's what to look for in a fishing vest (below) and some suggestions on selecting the necessary accessories (next page). Of course, the specific gear you need will depend on the type of fishing you do.

A good fishing vest has plenty of pockets with zippers or Velcro fasteners so they can be closed to prevent loss of gear. There should be a loop at the back of the collar so you can attach a landing net. Select a vest large enough that you can wear a layer of warm clothing beneath it.

Wading Staff

Common Accessories
for Stream-Trout Fishing

Wading Jacket

Fingerless
Gloves

Wading Belt

Portable Seine

Landing Net

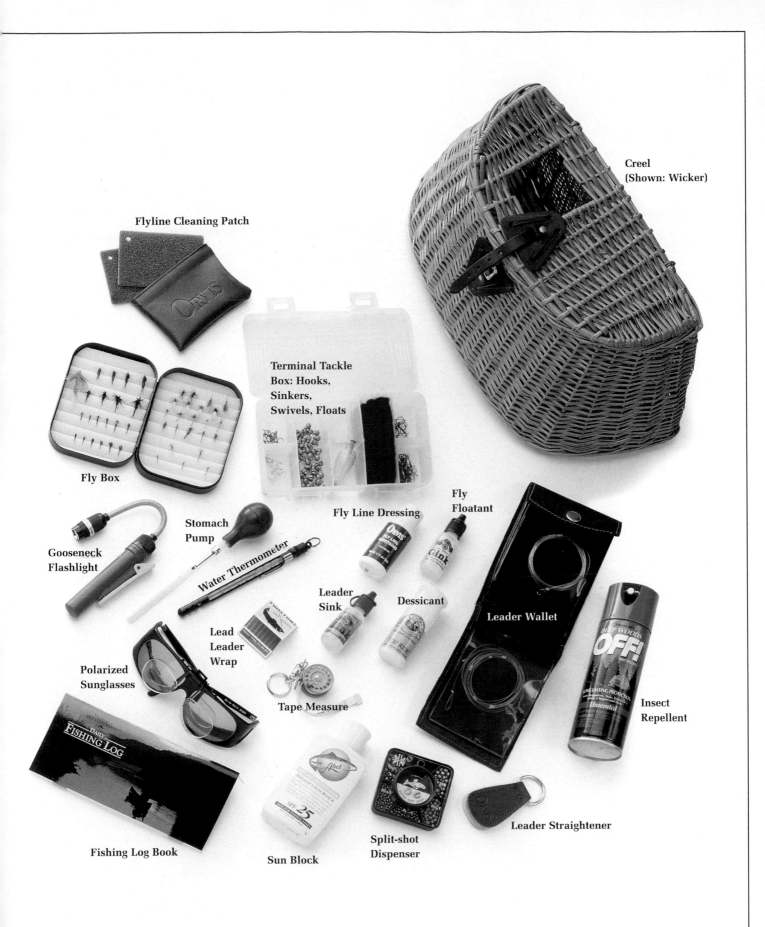

Flyline Cleaning Patch

Creel
(Shown: Wicker)

Terminal Tackle
Box: Hooks,
Sinkers,
Swivels, Floats

Fly Box

Fly Line Dressing

Fly
Floatant

Gooseneck
Flashlight

Stomach
Pump

Water Thermometer

Leader
Sink

Dessicant

Leader Wallet

Insect
Repellent

Lead
Leader
Wrap

Polarized
Sunglasses

Tape Measure

FISHING LOG

Fishing Log Book

Sun Block

Split-shot
Dispenser

Leader Straightener

STREAM-FISHING TECHNIQUES

The techniques for catching stream trout are as varied as the fish themselves and the waters they live in.

Drab clothing is a must for stream-trout fishing. If you wear a red cap, a white shirt or any other brightly-colored attire, your chances of sneaking up on trout undetected go way down.

A STEALTHY APPROACH

In order to survive in a stream environment, trout must learn to be super wary. They are quick to detect any unusual sound, vibration or movement that could signal the presence of predators like herons, kingfishers and fishermen.

Regardless of what fishing technique you use, stealth is of the utmost importance. Once you spook a trout, it isn't likely to bite for several hours no matter what your strategy.

Here are some tips for moving into a position where you can catch trout without them detecting you first.

Tips for Approaching Trout

Use trees, bushes or other streamside cover to conceal yourself. Whenever possible, try to stay in the shadows rather than in bright sunlight.

Stay low to keep out of the trout's window of vision (p. 11). Because of the way light rays entering the water are bent, the fish can see objects at a lower angle than would seem possible.

Avoid sloshing the water as you wade. Move your feet slowly, using short steps, and try not to disturb the water. If possible, wade upstream so the sediment you stir up does not drift over the fish.

FISHING WITH HARDWARE

In the eyes of a fly-fishing "purist," hardware ranks only a notch above live bait on the acceptability scale. But there is no arguing the fact that hardware catches big trout—and lots of them.

As trout grow larger, baitfish comprise a larger part of their diet, so it's not surprising that these hard-bodied, minnow-imitating lures are so effective.

There are three main types of hardware:

IN-LINE SPINNERS

These lures have long been a favorite of stream-trout anglers because even a slight current causes the blade to rotate on the straight wire shaft. The spinning blade produces plenty of vibration and flash, even at a very slow retrieve speed. If you wish, just hang a spinner in the current and let the moving water turn the blade.

In-line spinners come in two basic styles:

• **French Spinners**. These lures consist of a blade that rotates around the shaft on a clevis (a metal attachment device). Behind the blade is a weighted body and a treble hook, which may be dressed with feathers or a soft-plastic body. A French spinner emits intense vibrations, so it is an excellent choice in discolored water.

• **Sonic Spinners**. The design is much the same as that of a French Spinner, but the blade spins directly on the shaft, rather than on a clevis. Because the blade is convex on one end and concave on the other, it catches water and spins easily even in the slowest current. The vibrations produced, however, are not as intense as those of a French spinner.

Shyster

Popular French Spinners

Miracle Firemax

Mepps Aglia

Popular Sonic Spinners

Panther Martin

Worden's Rooster Tail

Vibric Rooster Tail

SPOONS

Anglers on good-sized trout streams rely heavily on spoons made of medium to thick metal, because they can be cast a long distance (even into a stiff wind) and will stay down in the current. Thin spoons are much less popular for stream fishing, although they are sometimes used in small, slow-moving waters.

Most spoons used for stream-trout fishing measure from 1½ to 3 inches in length. For best results, choose a spoon that's just heavy enough to barely tick bottom when you quarter your cast upstream and then make a slow retrieve. A ¼-ounce spoon may be heavy enough in a shallow, slow-moving stream, but in deeper, faster water, you may need a spoon weighing more than an ounce.

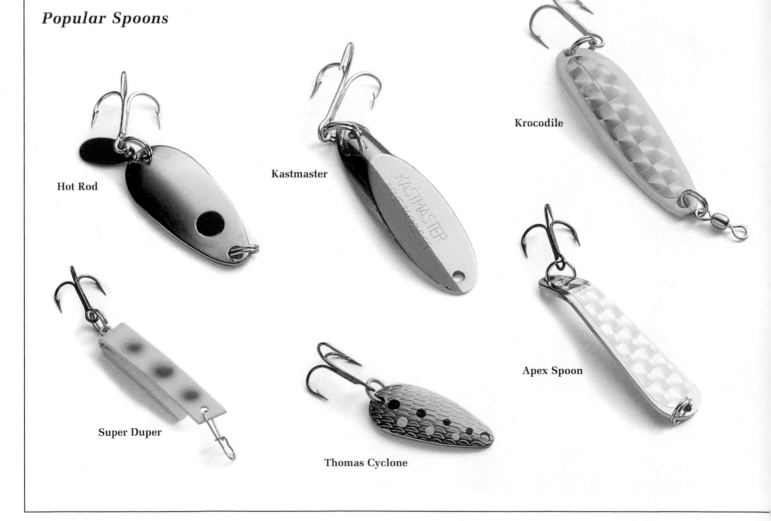

If your spoon does not have a split-ring for attaching the line, add one. This will vastly improve the lure's action, drawing more strikes.

Blue Fox Pixee Spoon

Popular Spoons

Hot Rod

Kastmaster

Krocodile

Super Duper

Thomas Cyclone

Apex Spoon

PLUGS

While spoons and spinners attract fish with flash and vibration, plugs add the element of realism. Some look almost exactly like shiners and other common stream minnows.

Here are the most popular plugs used for stream-trout:

•**Minnowbaits**. If you check the tackle box of most serious hardware fishermen, you'll find a selection of floating minnowbaits ranging from 2½ to 4 inches in length. These baits, which come in shallow-running and deep-diving models, have an extremely lifelike wobble.

Sinking minnowbaits work well for fishing deep water, but their wobble is less intense than that of floaters.

•**Crankbaits**. These diving plugs get down in a hurry, so they are a good choice for fishing deep pools and runs. But they have a wider wobble than a minnowbait and are not as representative of a stream's natural forage.

•**Trolling Plugs**. You can troll with a minnowbait or crankbait, but many anglers prefer plugs designed specifically for trolling.

Most of these plugs have a wide "bill" that gives them an erratic, darting action when trolled. They are difficult to cast because of their light weight and the wind resistance a bill creates.

Recommended Tackle

A 6- to 7-foot medium-power spinning rod with a fairly light tip is a good choice for casting minnowbaits. Pair it with a medium-weight spinning reel spooled with 6- to 8-pound mono. A 7½- to 8½-foot bait-casting rod with a soft tip works well for fishing trolling plugs in large rivers. Use a level-wind reel with 10- to 12-pound mono.

Plugs can be tied directly onto the line, using a loop knot. But most anglers prefer to attach them with a small clip.

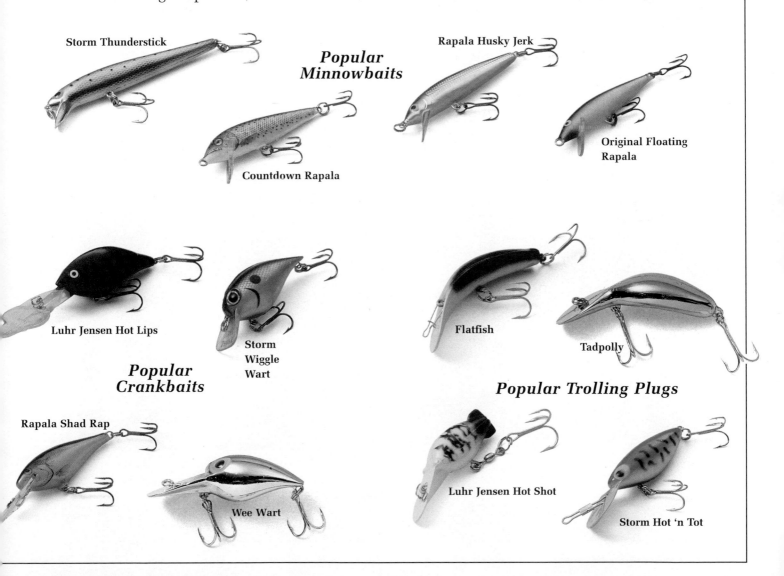

Storm Thunderstick

Popular Minnowbaits

Rapala Husky Jerk

Countdown Rapala

Original Floating Rapala

Luhr Jensen Hot Lips

Storm Wiggle Wart

Popular Crankbaits

Rapala Shad Rap

Wee Wart

Flatfish

Tadpolly

Popular Trolling Plugs

Luhr Jensen Hot Shot

Storm Hot 'n Tot

TECHNIQUES FOR FISHING WITH HARDWARE

There are times when a novice can pick up a spinning rod, aimlessly heave a big spoon toward the opposite bank and immediately hook a good-sized trout. But more often, hardware fishing requires some finesse and an understanding of what lures and presentations are likely to work best in a particular situation.

Hardware fishermen rely primarily on the following methods:

WADING

Most small- to medium-sized streams and some large, shallow streams can be fished effectively by wading while quartering casts upstream to retrieve your lure through prime pools and runs.

A beginning hardware fisherman soon learns to compensate for the moving water. If you cast straight across the current, for example, the water will catch your line right away, creating a "belly" and pulling your lure rapidly downstream. You'll miss the zone you were targeting and the lure will be moving so fast and running so shallow that the fish will ignore it.

If you angle your casts upstream, however, the lure will have a chance to sink or dive before the current catches the line. It will run deeper and at a much slower speed, giving you a much more natural presentation.

How far you angle your casts upstream depends on water depth, current speed and the lure you're using. The straighter upstream you cast, the deeper your lure will track. On the other hand, if you're bumping bottom too much, angle your casts farther downstream so the current gives your lure more lift.

When casting to a specific target, such as an eddy behind a boulder, cast beyond and well upstream of the spot. If you cast right into the pocket, you may spook the fish, and by the time the lure gets deep enough, the current will have swept it away.

How to Determine Casting Angle

Correct. *Angle your cast far enough upstream that your line does not develop much belly until the very end of the retrieve. This way, the lure stays deep enough for trout to see it, and it moves slowly enough for them to grab it.*

Wrong. *If you angle your cast too far downstream, your line will immediately develop a belly that will rapidly sweep the lure well downstream of its desired path. During the last part of the retrieve, the lure will be moving upstream.*

DRIFTING

Although the majority of hardware fishing is done while wading or casting from shore, there will be times when these methods won't put the lure in the fish zone. The stream may simply be too large for you to reach the most productive areas, or the current may be so fast that your lure is quickly swept away.

By casting from a drifting boat, however, you can easily reach the best pools and runs. And with the boat drifting at the same speed as the current, the effects of moving water are minimized.

Drifting enables you to cover much more water than you can by wading but, if you find an exceptionally productive spot, you can toss out an anchor and work the area more thoroughly.

As you drift, plan your casts to cover any obvious trout lies, such as deep pools and runs, eddies, pockets, current seams, fallen trees, logjams and boulders. But remember that not all trout lies are visible, so it pays to thoroughly cover the water.

In most cases, you'll want to drift down the center of the stream and cast to both sides. But the current is usually swifter in the center than along the edges, so you'll normally have to angle your casts downstream (below).

Another way to solve the problem is to lower a heavy chain off the bow and let it drag bottom as you drift. The chain will keep the bow pointed upstream, even if there is a crosswind, and it will slow your drift speed to reduce fishing-line drag, allowing you to better cover the water.

When drifting, you'll encounter a wide variety of water types, so it pays to have at least two rods rigged with different lures. When you come to a deep pool, for example, grab a rod with a deep-diving crankbait. When you come to a riffle, pick up a rod with a minnowbait or spinner.

The best way to drift a stream is to launch your boat at one access site and use a second vehicle to pick it up at another site several miles downstream. This way, you can fish all of the prime water in that reach without having to run back upstream when you're done and risk damaging your outboard.

Drifting Tips

When casting from the center of the stream toward the edges, angle your casts downstream to compensate for the faster midstream current. With the boat at position A, for example, you should angle your cast as shown. Then, by the time the boat has drifted to position B, you will have completed your retrieve (dotted line) with only a small downstream bow and very little drag.

A McKenzie River boat is ideal for drifting because one angler can control the drift speed with the oars while another casts. This minimizes the effects of drag.

TROLLING

An extremely popular technique in many large western rivers and in some Great Lakes tributaries, trolling not only allows you to cover a lot of water, but it also enables you to fish with multiple lines (where legal).

To troll effectively, you need a long stretch of relatively deep water with slow to moderate current. Trolling is not a good way to fish a river with swift current or numerous riffles or rapids.

There are three primary methods of trolling for stream trout; each has a slightly different purpose:

• **Upstream Trolling**. To troll in a stretch of slow-moving water of uniform depth, simply toss out your lure and begin motoring upstream. In most cases you'll have to troll very slowly; otherwise the current will force your lure to the surface and cause it to skip.

To prevent trolling over the fish and spooking them, try to troll in an S-pattern. This way your lures will not follow the exact path of the boat. Or use side planers (p. 98) which prevent spooking and enable you to cover a wide swath of water.

• **"Backtrolling."** Steelhead anglers commonly use this method for fishing specific deep runs or pools, especially when the water is cold and the fish are inactive. The technique involves trolling into the current while allowing the boat to slip slowly backwards or downstream (opposite page). Because the lure reaches the fish before the boat does, spooking is not as much of a problem as it would be if you trolled upstream. The technique is also called "slipping" or "Hotshotting," in reference to a popular plug used for the method, the Luhr Jensen Hot Shot.

The key to successful backtrolling is keeping the boat drifting more slowly than the current; otherwise the lure will have very little action.

The "drop-back" technique (opposite) is a variation of the backtrolling method. Instead of using your motor and slipping, just anchor the boat and keep letting out line to cover the run.

• **Downstream Trolling**. This technique is not as common as the others, but it works well in slow current. The trick is to motor downstream fast enough to give your lure the desired action. With a spinner or small minnowbait, you'll get the right action by trolling just slightly faster than the current; with a crankbait or spoon, you'll have to go considerably faster.

Downstream trolling enables you to keep your line in the water most of the time. Instead of trolling upstream and then (when you finish your run) pulling up your line to motor back downstream to make another run, just keep your line in the water and troll back down.

The "Backtrolling" Technique

Motor to the upper end of a deep pool or run and hold the boat in position while letting out enough line to get the lure down to the fish (usually 60-70 feet). Use a long rod (at least 8 feet) with a light tip; this way, you can easily monitor the plug's action.

Let out the rest of your lines, put your rods in rod holders and then let the boat begin slipping downstream. Watch your depth finder closely and try to keep the boat in the deepest part of the slot. Steer right to direct the boat to the right and vice versa.

The "Drop-Back" Technique

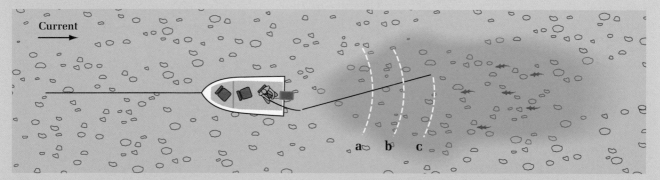

Anchor your boat at the head of a long pool or run and let out about 25 feet of line. Hold your rod motionless for 30 to 45 seconds; the lure will (a) wiggle enticingly in the current and swing from side to side. Then (b) let out about 3 feet of line and repeat the procedure. Continue letting out line in (c) 3-foot intervals until the entire pool or run has been covered.

How to Fish with Side Planers

Side planers are small wooden or plastic devices that attach to your line for the purpose of carrying your lure to the side of the boat's wake to prevent spooking wary fish, including trout. By trolling with several lines rigged with side planers, you can cover a swath of water more than 100 feet wide.

Side planers used in trout fishing are usually rigged so that when a fish strikes, the line releases from the board, which then slides down the line until it hits a barrel swivel several feet above the lure. This way the angler can fight the fish without too much resistance from the board.

1 Let out the desired amount of line, usually 75 to 100 feet. Then attach the line to the release device on the board. Clip the rear snap over the line.

2 Let the board plane to the side, carrying the line and lure with it. Place your rod in a rod holder.

3 When a fish strikes, the board will slide to the end of the line, stopping above the lure. Fight the fish carefully; if it gets leverage against the board, it could break your line.

Use a side planer to reach trout in midstream when fishing from shore. Just make a short downstream cast, attach your line to the board as shown on the opposite page and feed line to let the board carry the line out. If desired, you can slowly walk downstream to "backtroll."

"Burn" a floating minnowbait or spinner through a riffle to catch the active feeders. Stand well downstream of the riffle, aim your cast to land upstream of the riffle and reel rapidly. If there is a trout present, it will usually strike on the first or second cast.

Plan your casts to prevent any fish you hook from spooking other fish. Your strategy should be to first work the cover that is both closest to you and farthest downstream. Otherwise a hooked fish will disturb the other spots. In the situation shown above, spots 1-4 should be worked in that order.

When trolling in moving water, always check your lure's action by letting out a few feet of line and watching how the lure wiggles in the current. If the action does not look right, adjust your trolling speed or try a different lure.

JIG FISHING

The leadhead jig may well be the most under-rated of all trout lures. Although jigs have never gained widespread popularity in trout-fishing circles, their effectiveness should come as no surprise. They sink quickly to the bottom, where big trout live, and they look like many big-trout foods including minnows, leeches, crayfish, larval insects and salmon eggs.

Jigs are also quite versatile. You can fish them with a twitch-and-pause retrieve, jig them vertically or drift them in the same manner as you would a nymph (p. 132).

Twitch-and-Pause. To fish a deep pool or run, tie on a 1/16- to 1/4-ounce jig and angle your cast upstream. Let the jig sink to the bottom and then retrieve it in short twitches followed by pauses. As the jig sinks after each pause, be sure to keep your line taut; otherwise you won't feel the take.

Vertical Jigging. An option for deep pools and runs in large rivers, vertical jigging involves lowering a 3/8- to 1-ounce leadhead jig or other jigging lure to the bottom, lifting it a few inches and then lowering it again on a taut line. Set the hook when you feel any twitch or tug.

Drifting. When trout are feeding in a riffle, cast a microjig (1/32 to 1/100 ounce) well upstream and allow it to drift through the fast-moving water. Hold your rod tip high and keep the line taut to detect strikes. Or use a strike indicator (opposite).

Recommended Tackle

For the twitch-and-pause retrieve, use a 5 1/4- to 6-foot medium-power spinning rod with a fast tip and a medium-size spinning reel spooled with 4- to 8-pound mono. A 6- to 7-foot, medium-power, fast-tip baitcasting outfit with 10- to 14-pound mono is a better choice for vertically jigging. For drifting microjigs, you'll need a 4 1/2- to 5 1/2-foot ultralight, soft-tip spinning outfit spooled with extra-limp 2- to 4-pound mono.

Mister Twister Meeny

The Natural Bucktail Jig

Popular Jigs

Feather Tail Jig

Marabou Jig

Blue Fox Micro Jig

Turner Jones Micro Jig

Swedish Pimple

Popular Microjigs

Popular Jigging Lures

Cicada

Incredible Jig

Jig-Fishing Tips

When drifting microjigs, use a strike indicator to detect takes. If you see the indicator twitch or hesitate, set the hook.

Tip your jig with live bait, such as a small minnow or half a nightcrawler, for extra appeal. When tipping, be sure to use a sparsely-dressed jig.

FISHING WITH NATURAL BAIT

Worms are the primary weapon of many beginning trout anglers, and even veteran fly fishermen have been known to put on some "garden hackle" when the going gets tough.

There are times when trout will attack almost any kind of lure you toss into the water. But they're usually much more selective; they closely inspect your offering and, if it doesn't look real, ignore it.

Natural bait is the ultimate in realism, assuming it is hooked and presented properly. But the attraction of natural bait is much more than visual—it also appeals to the trout's highly developed sense of smell.

When the water is high and muddy and the visibility is near zero, trout cannot possibly see hardware or flies, but they can pick up and track the scent of natural bait.

Natural bait is also the best choice during cold-water periods when the insect hatch is minimal. And natural bait is hard to beat for catching trophy trout, which tend to be extra-fussy about what they eat.

Despite the unique appeal of natural bait, many anglers don't catch as many trout as they should because they use the wrong terminal tackle. In most cases, for example, there is no need for a large float or heavy sinker. A small hook

Many a nice trout has been fooled by live bait.

and a split shot will normally do the job.

Another common problem is hooking the bait improperly. If the bait is not hooked the right way, it will look unnatural and you may lose it when you cast.

Natural bait is not a good choice if you will be releasing your trout, because the fish often swallow the hook. If

that happens and you want to release the fish, don't try to remove the hook; just cut the line. The hook will eventually dissolve.

Before using natural bait, check the regulations for the stream you're fishing to be

sure it is legal. The use of live baitfish is prohibited in many trout streams for fear of introduction of unwanted fish species, and because live bait is so effective for catching trout.

Shown on the following pages are the most common types of natural bait used for stream trout.

Popular Types of Live Bait

Worms

Garden worms probably account for more stream trout than any other type of natural bait. They will catch trout of any size. If you're targeting large trout, however, a nightcrawler is a better choice.

Worms are effective at any time of year, but they work especially well in early spring when the water is cold, high and muddy. Another good time to use worms is after a heavy rain when rising water washes worms into the stream.

Hook a crawler through the middle with a size 6 to 8 hook or break it in half and hook the broken end.

Hook a garden worm by threading it partway onto a size 6 to 10 hook. You can also hook it once through the middle, as you would a crawler, or hook it 2 or 3 times so only the tail is left dangling.

Night Crawlers

Garden Worms

Minnows

Almost any kind of live minnow from 1½ to 3 inches long will catch trout throughout the year. Simply hook your minnow through the lips (top) with a size 4 or 6 short-shank bait hook.

Anglers fishing deep, slow pools often rely on freshly killed minnows or cut bait (bottom), which take advantage of the scavenging habits of large trout, particularly browns.

Aquatic Insects

Because immature aquatic insects comprise such a large portion of a trout's diet, they make excellent bait. The toughest immature forms, such as waterworms (cranefly larvae), hellgrammites (dobsonfly larvae) and stonefly nymphs, are most popular.

A hellgrammite (shown) is normally hooked under the collar with a size 4 to 8 light-wire hook; a waterworm (inset), through the tough portion of the tail with a size 4 to 8 light-wire hook. A stonefly nymph (not shown) is usually hooked under the collar with a size 8 or 10 light-wire hook.

Adult aquatic insects and delicate immature forms, such as mayfly nymphs and caddisfly larvae, are sometimes used for bait, but they're difficult to keep on the hook.

Terrestrial Insects

Grasshoppers, crickets and other terrestrial insects are commonly blown into streams, where they make an easy meal for trout. Even when no aquatic insects are hatching, trout will feed on terrestrial forms.

Of all terrestrial insects, grasshoppers are most commonly used as bait. Grasshoppers and crickets can be hooked under the collar (inset) or threaded on (left) using a size 6 to 10, long-shank, light-wire hook (inset).

Larval terrestrial insects such as waxworms (bee moth larvae) and maggots or "spikes" (fly larvae), are rapidly gaining popularity among trout fishermen. They're normally hooked through the head (2 or 3 at a time) with a size 10 or 12 short-shank, light-wire hook as shown.

Crustaceans

Small crayfish (less than 3 inches long) are good bait for large trout, particularly browns. Hook them through the tail using a size 2 or 4 short-shank bait hook, as shown.

Smaller trout would have a hard time swallowing a whole crayfish, but you can catch them on a crayfish tail hooked from the bottom up with a size 4 or 6 hook.

Scuds, a common food item for stream trout, can be found clinging to submerged weeds. They have not gained widespread popularity as bait because they're difficult to keep on the hook. Anglers who use them thread two or three onto a size 12 to 14 light-wire hook.

Single Salmon Eggs

Dolly Varden have gained the unenviable reputation as being predators on the eggs of trout and salmon. But the fact is, all trout and salmon feed on each others' eggs to some degree. So it's not surprising that fresh trout and salmon eggs make excellent stream-trout bait.

Salmon eggs are larger than trout eggs, so they're the best choice for rigging individually, although trout eggs will also work. To fish a single egg you'll need a size 10 to 14 salmon-egg hook, which has an extra-short shank and a turned-up eye. Just (1) push the hook through the side of the egg, (2) turn the hook 180 degrees and (3) bury the point in the opposite side of the egg.

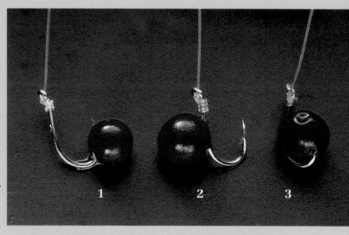

Grocery/Prepared Baits

Even if the bait shop isn't open, you can still get some good trout bait at the corner grocery store. Trout are commonly caught on whole-kernel corn, cheese balls, marshmallows and even baked beans.

Trout anglers also have good success on a variety of moldable, scent-impregnated baits and preformed nuggets.

All these grocery/prepared baits work best for freshly stocked trout, probably because the fish confuse them with hatchery food pellets. These baits are much less effective for wild trout or stocked trout that have become acclimated to a stream and its natural food.

How to Make a Spawn Bag

To make a spawn bag (1) put some eggs on a 3-inch square piece of nylon mesh, (2) gather the corners and then wrap the base of the bag with thread, (3) tie the thread securely and push a size 4 to 8 short-shank hook into the bag, leaving the point exposed.

How to Make an Egg Loop

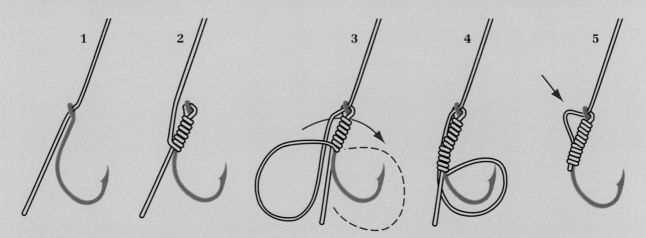

To make an egg loop, you'll need a hook with a turned-up eye and a 2-foot piece of mono. Then (1) push your line through the eye; (2) make 6 wraps around the shank and tag end and hold the wraps with your fingers; (3) push the other end of the line through the eye, leaving a loop; (4) wrap one leg of the loop over the other leg and the tag end about 6 times, as shown; (5) snug up the knot by pulling on the line, then open the loop (arrow) by pushing on the line. Cut a section of eggs from a fresh skein (p. 109), put them into the loop and snug up the line.

Collect burrowing larvae such as waterworms and mayfly nymphs by digging through mud, sticks and leaves in a beaver dam.

Shake a clump of aquatic vegetation over a pail of water to collect scuds. Or sweep a fine mesh net or screen through the weeds.

Kick over rocks and then use a long-handled dip net to catch any larval insects that are dislodged and drift downstream.

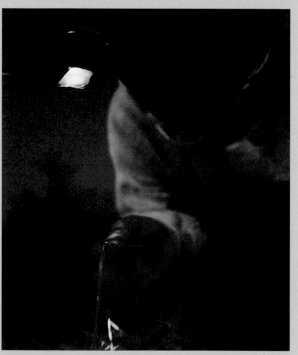

Find nightcrawlers using a flashlight with a piece of red cellophane over the lens. The worms may retreat back down their holes when they see a white light, but a red light doesn't affect them as much.

Tips for Carrying & Keeping Live Bait

Attach a metal worm box to your belt for carrying garden worms or night crawlers. This model rides upside down; this way, the worms are right on top when you flip it over.

Strap a small minnow bucket with a perforated lid to your waders. Fresh water flowing in through the holes keeps the bait alive.

Use a commercial cricket dispenser to carry crickets or grasshoppers. Be sure to select the type that dispenses the insects one at a time.

Carry enough insect larvae for a day of fishing in a plastic container filled with damp moss. Most larvae will live out of water for several days.

Preserve salmon eggs by cutting a fresh skein into ¾-inch cubes (left), rolling the cubes in powdered borax and then putting them in a baby food jar containing a layer of borax. Shake the covered jar to thoroughly coat the cubes (middle). The eggs can be refrigerated for several weeks or frozen for long-term storage. For a day of fishing, carry the preserved eggs in a flip-top egg dispenser that attaches to your belt (right).

Fresh salmon eggs or spawn bags are one of the top drift-fishing baits.

DRIFT-FISHING

Whether you're after half-pound brookies or 15-pound steelhead, drift-fishing with natural bait is one of the most effective stream-fishing methods.

Not only does drift-fishing enable you to cover a lot of water, it presents the bait in a lifelike manner so trout mistake it for food that is drifting naturally with the current.

The most popular baits for drift-fishing are nightcrawlers and salmon eggs, but you can drift-fish with most any kind of live bait. Delicate insect baits, however, may be diffi-

cult to keep on the hook, especially on a rocky bottom. Some anglers even drift-fish with grocery baits.

Drift-fishing works best in a deep riffle or run where there is enough current to keep the bait moving. It is not recommended for fishing pools with little or no current.

Once you find a likely riffle or run, look for the deepest slot and then quarter your cast upstream at a 45- to 60-degree angle to the current. The key to success is to keep your bait drifting along the bottom at the same speed as the current. To accomplish

this, you must attach precisely the right amount of weight. If you don't use enough weight, the current will lift your bait too far off bottom; if you use too much weight, the bait will drift too slowly and look unnatural.

To cover a riffle or run thoroughly, you may have to drift your bait through it many times. The average angler has a tendency to make his first cast a long one, but that's usually a mistake. Should you hook a fish on a long cast, the struggle will probably spook any fish that are closer to you. Instead, cover the water closest to you first and the water farthest from you last.

When a trout takes the bait, you may feel a sharp tug or tap but, more often, the bait will simply stop moving. The best policy is to set the hook whenever you feel anything out of the ordinary.

When trout are taking insects on the surface, try drifting your bait with no weight. This method, which works particularly well in late summer and early fall, is sometimes called *freelining*.

Recommended Tackle

You can drift-fish for small- to medium-sized trout using a 6- to 7-foot medium-power spinning outfit with 4- to 6-pound-test mono.

For steelhead or other large trout, you'll need an 8- to 9-foot, medium-heavy- to heavy-power, long-handled "steelhead-class" baitcasting outfit with 8 to 17-pound-test abrasion-resistant mono.

The basic drift-fishing rig consists of a bait hook with one or more split shot 8 to 12 inches above it (top). For fishing on a snaggy bottom, however, use a dropper rig (bottom). This way, the split shot will pull off the dropper when you get snagged, saving the rest of your rig.

How to Drift-Fish

Angle your cast upstream to (a) the closest part of a likely riffle or run. Hold your rod tip high as your bait drifts, keeping the line taut until the bait is well downstream of your position. Make several drifts through the same zone and then reel up and make (b) a slightly longer cast at the same angle. Repeat the procedure until the entire riffle or run has been thoroughly covered (c and beyond).

How to Freeline

Thread a grasshopper, cricket or other adult insect onto a long-shank, light-wire hook. The insect should float on or just beneath the surface.

Fish along a grassy bank where grasshoppers and other insects commonly fall into the stream. Trout lie at the base of the grass waiting for an easy meal.

Feed line so your bait drifts naturally with the current and creates no drag. Let the bait drift for about 25 or 30 feet, then reel in and drift it again. Watch the bait closely and set the hook immediately when a trout sucks it in.

How to Make a Yarn Fly

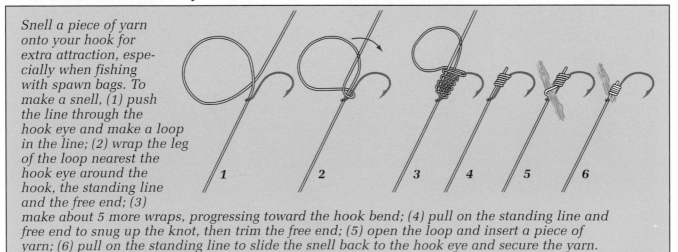

Snell a piece of yarn onto your hook for extra attraction, especially when fishing with spawn bags. To make a snell, (1) push the line through the hook eye and make a loop in the line; (2) wrap the leg of the loop nearest the hook eye around the hook, the standing line and the free end; (3) make about 5 more wraps, progressing toward the hook bend; (4) pull on the standing line and free end to snug up the knot, then trim the free end; (5) open the loop and insert a piece of yarn; (6) pull on the standing line to slide the snell back to the hook eye and secure the yarn. Some avid steelhead anglers use the yarn, by itself, without the eggs.

1   2   3   4   5   6

Drift-fish a short run using a long fly rod rigged with monofilament line. With a long rod you can simply pick up the line and flick it back upstream when the bait reaches the end of the run rather than taking time to reel up and cast again.

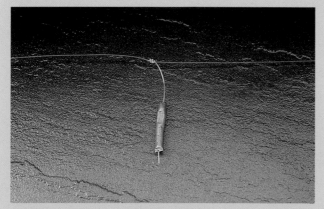

Use a piece of pencil lead instead of a split shot when you need more weight. Pinch the ends of the weight to keep it on the dropper. When the sinker snags, a sharp tug will pull it off of the line and free the rig.

Thread a floater, such as a "corkie," onto your line before tying on your hook. A floater not only reduces the number of snags, it acts as an attractor. Some floaters are designed to spin for even more attraction.

Floating prevents a large belly from forming in your line, so your bait drifts naturally along the bottom.

FLOATING

The best way to scout the trout potential of a river is by floating. And on large rivers that are too deep to wade or have limited shoreline access, floating may be the only effective way to fish trout.

The usual procedure requires at least two anglers, each with a vehicle, along with a shallow-draft boat. The first step is to leave one vehicle at a downstream access site. Then the two anglers drive upstream to another access site, launch the boat and spend the day floating back to the downstream site.

Along the way, they have ample opportunity to explore the best trout-holding spots, and experiment with different presentations.

Floating also gives anglers an edge they would not have if they were shorefishing or wading. Because the boat and bait are moving at pretty much the same speed as the current, a belly does not

form in your line to create drag. And there is no need to continually reel up your line and cast; just leave your bait on the bottom and

adjust your depth as the boat floats along.

If you're after steelhead or other large trout, floating offers yet another big advantage. When the fish feels the hook and rockets downstream into the next pool, all you have to do is follow it with the boat rather than run after it in your waders and stumble over slippery rocks.

You can float-fish with the same baits and rigs used for drift-fishing (p. 110), although there are some special float-fishing rigs (opposite). The information on these pages applies mainly to floating with natural bait, but the floating technique also works well for fishing with hardware and flies.

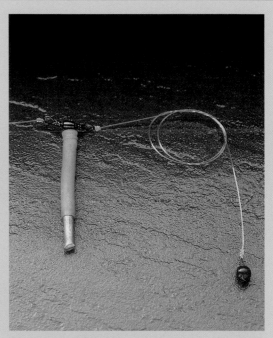

Splice a crankbait with the hooks removed into your line, leaving a trailer about 3 feet long. The crankbait will pull the bait to the bottom, give it extra action and serve as an attractor.

Use a surgical-tubing rig on a snaggy bottom. Just push a piece of pencil lead into the tubing. Then, should the pencil lead get snagged, it will pull out so you don't lose the whole rig.

To work eddies and pockets along the edge of fast current, one angler slows the boat's drift while the other casts to the upstream end of the slower water and lets the current sweep the bait downstream.

To work deep pools and runs, control the boat with oars or a small motor to keep it drifting at the same speed as the current. This way your line stays vertical, enabling you to easily feel the bottom and detect bites.

STILL-FISHING

In many trout streams, the biggest trout of the year are caught by novice anglers "soaking" some type of natural or prepared bait on the bottom.

But still-fishing is not just for beginners. A surprising number of experienced trophy hunters rely heavily on the technique because they know that the biggest trout are lazy. These monsters spend most of their time lying motionless in deep pools, waiting for the current to deliver them a sizable meal.

Big trout also tend to be scavengers. They are just as likely to grab a dead baitfish (or a piece of one) as they are a live one. This explains why many trophy fishermen rely on cut bait.

Recommended Tackle

You can still-fish for stream trout with practically any kind of tackle, but most anglers use a light spinning rod from 6 to 6½ feet in length and a lightweight spinning reel spooled with 4- to 6-pound-test mono.

Most still-fishing involves finding a deep pool that can be fished comfortably from the bank, tossing out your line and waiting for a bite.

The rigging is simple: Just tie on a hook and pinch on a split shot or two. Use just enough weight to keep your bait from drifting. If there is too much current to hold bottom with a split-shot rig, use a slip-sinker rig. This way your bait will stay put, yet a fish can grab it and swim off without feeling resistance.

When you need to place your bait in a tight spot or reach trout holding beneath an undercut, try a technique called "dabbling." Let a few feet of line dangle from the end of your rod and then dip your bait vertically into a slackwater pocket along the bank or along the edge of an undercut (opposite).

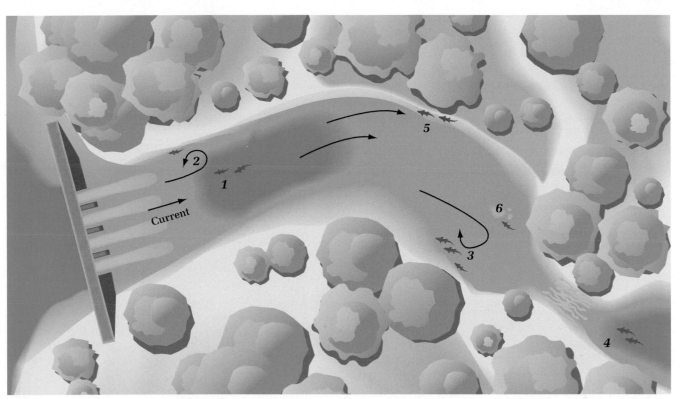

Prime spots for still-fishing include (1) deep pool, (2) eddy below a low-head dam, (3) eddy below a point and (4) plunge pool below a waterfall. For dabbling, try (5) a section of undercut bank and (6) a small eddy below a boulder.

Still-Fishing Tips

Look for a spot, usually along an outside bend, where the current cuts into the bank, creating an undercut. Dabble your bait over the lip of the undercut, hold it motionless for a few seconds then move on to the next spot.

Fish your bait on a floating jig head to keep it off bottom so it will be more visible. The bait will also have more movement as the floating head sways gently in the current.

FLY FISHING

For centuries, anglers have been infatuated with the idea of outwitting wary stream trout with a bit of fur or feathers tied onto a hook. And even though fly fishing is one of the oldest forms of angling, its popularity is still growing.

Throwing a fly line on an uncrowded stream, for some, is the ultimate means of relaxation. Others enjoy the challenge of observing hatching insects and trying to tie flies that mimic them. But most take up fly fishing for a very simple reason: It's a highly effective trout-catching method.

When trout are feeding on a particular insect form, as they so often do, nothing is as effective as a fly that resembles the natural. During a heavy insect hatch, a hardware fisherman may land a trout or two but a competent fly angler will be hooked up constantly.

Although some fly fishermen go to great lengths to select a fly that looks exactly like the real thing, such precision is rarely necessary. In most cases, a fly that gives a good approximation of the natural will do the job (below).

Not all flies, however, are intended to represent insects. Some imitate minnows, crayfish, scuds, leeches, frogs and even salmon eggs. Other flies are classified as attractors; they don't really represent anything a trout would ever see—or eat. They arouse a trout's curiosity with their color, flash or shape.

Regardless of their design, the vast majority of flies have one thing in common: They are too light to cast with ordinary spinning or baitcasting gear. Fly-fishing gear, however, will easily propel a nearly weightless fly because you're casting the line itself, not what's on the end of it.

Many anglers have heard how difficult it is to cast a fly, so they're reluctant to try it. But as you will see, it's really not as difficult as you may have thought.

On the pages that follow, we'll give you the information you need to start fly fishing for stream trout. You'll learn how to rig your line and leader, how to make the essential casts and how to present the various types of floating and sinking flies.

> **Recommended Tackle**
>
> Most fly fishing for stream trout is done with a 2- to 6-weight fly rod and a double-taper or weight-forward line. For large trout, you may need a 7- to 9-weight rod. The flotation of your line and length of your leader depend on the specific type of fly fishing you will be doing.

There is no need to use an exact imitation of the natural, but try to select a fly of the approximate size, shape and color.

Stream-Fishing Techniques

RIGGING FLY TACKLE

You can buy the most expensive fly rod and reel and stock your fly box with every conceivable fly pattern, but if you don't rig your line and leader properly, all of your efforts will be wasted.

The first step is to select the right line and leader for the type of fishing you'll be doing. Refer to pages 74-75 for information on choosing your fly line; 76-77 for choosing your leader.

Although you can attach your entire leader to your fly line using a tube knot, most anglers prefer to attach only a short connector made of 25- to 30-pound test extra-stiff mono with a perfection loop at the end. This way you can change leaders in only a few seconds using a loop-to-loop connection.

The next step is tying on your fly. You can attach any fly with a double-clinch knot, but may anglers prefer a loop knot for attaching subsurface flies. A loop knot gives the fly more action, allowing it to swing freely in the current.

All the knots needed for attaching leaders and flies are shown below and on the opposite page.

Before you start fishing, check your leader to make sure it is not badly coiled. If it is, it won't cast properly and the coils may prevent you from feeling strikes. To remove the coils, pull the leader through a leader straightener (p. 85).

It's also a good idea to check your fly line. If it is dirty or cracked, it won't slide easily through the line guides and your casts will fall short. Clean and lubricate the line with fly line cleaner.

Attaching Mono Connector to Fly Line—Tube Knot

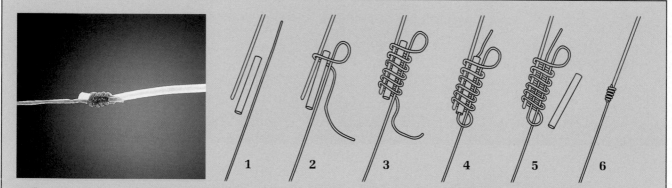

Tube Knot: *(1) Lay a small plastic drinking straw alongside the end of the fly line; (2) wrap the leader butt around the fly line, the straw and the standing portion of the leader; (3) make about 5 wraps, winding toward the end of the fly line; (4) push the butt of the leader back through the straw; (5) carefully remove the straw; (6) pull on both ends of the leader to snug up the knot.*

Making Loops in Mono Connector and Leader Butt—Perfection Loop

Perfection Loop: *(1) Make a loop by passing the tag end behind the standing line; (2) pass the tag end around and then behind the first loop to form a second loop; (3) bring the tag end between the two loops, as shown; (4) pull the second loop through the first loop; (5) snug up the knot by pulling on the loop and the standing line and then trim the tag end.*

Connecting Leader to Mono Connector—Loop-to-Loop Connection

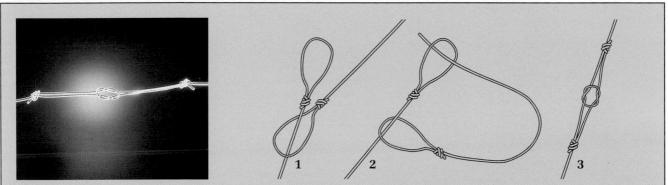

Loop-to-Loop Connection: *Make a perfection loop (see previous page) both in the mono connector on your fly line and in the butt of the leader. Then (1) pass the loop in the leader over the loop in the connector, (2) push the end of the leader through the loop in the connector and (3) snug up the knot by pulling both the leader and the connector. When you want to change leaders, just push on both lines to loosen the knot.*

Attaching Line to Fly—Double-Clinch (Trilene) Knot

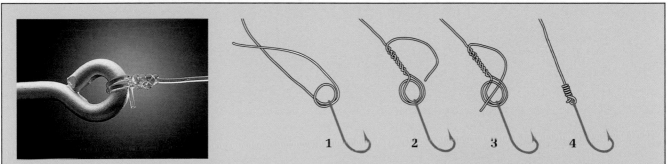

Double-Clinch Knot (Trilene Knot): *(1) Form a double loop by passing the free end through the cye of the fly twice, (2) wrap the free end around the standing line 4-5 times, (3) pass the free end through the double loop, (4) pull on both the standing line and the hook to snug up the knot. (Plain hook used here for clarity.)*

Attaching Line to Fly—Loop Knot

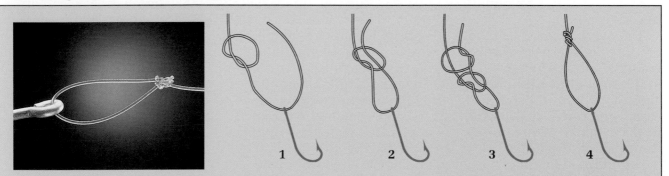

Loop Knot: *(1) Make an overhand knot near the end of the line and put the free end through the eye of the fly; (2) pass the free end through the overhand knot; (3) with the free end, make an overhand knot around the standing line (where you tie the second overhand determines the size of the loop); (4) tighten the overhand knots and pull the standing line to snug up the knot. (Plain hook used here for clarity.)*

Move your wrist and forearm on a level plane (arrow) to keep your casting loops tight. Wide loops (inset) will shorten your casts.

BASIC FLY CASTING

It may take years to learn all the finer points of fly casting, but you can learn the basic cast—and start catching trout—after only a few hours of practice.

The overhead cast, shown on the opposite page, forms the basis for most other types of fly casting. Use it to make short- to medium-distance casts, which will get you by in the majority of stream-trout-fishing situations.

Beginning fly casters are often frustrated when they try to make a powerful casting stroke but the line piles up in front of them, falling well short of its target. They soon learn that timing, not power, is the key to successful fly casting.

Remember that every casting stroke requires a gradual application of power. When you pick the line up off the water to make a backcast, you start with a slow, smooth stroke and accelerate into a much faster "speed stroke." The same principle applies on the forward casting stroke.

Another common mistake is pivoting your elbow rather than moving your forearm and wrist on a level plane (above). When you pivot your elbow, your rod tip will move in an arc, causing your casting loops to open too wide and shorten your casts.

Once you're comfortable with the overhead cast, practice making *false casts*. Instead of letting your forward cast fall to the water, make another backcast (or several more). While your line is in the air you can strip off additional line to lengthen your cast. Or you can adjust your casting angle if it looks like the cast is off target.

Learning the basic overhead cast will help you develop the "feel" necessary for handling fly line. Then you will have the confidence to begin experimenting with other types of casts, which are shown later in this chapter.

The Overhead Cast

1 *Strip off as much line as you think you'll need. Let it either pile neatly at your feet or float downstream with the current. Point your rod in the direction you wish to cast, then lift the rod and smoothly accelerate until all of the line is moving.*

2 *Propel the line into the backcast with a short, fast, speed stroke. This causes the rod to bend and generates enough power to draw the line backward.*

3 *Stop the rod just past the vertical and allow a loop to form as the line shoots backward.*

4 *Wait until the backcast unrolls into a narrow, J-shaped loop.*

5 *Stroke the rod forward, beginning slowly and then accelerating sharply; stop it abruptly at the position shown. The line should shoot forward and settle gently to the water. Lower the rod tip to begin fishing.*

DRY-FLY FISHING

Judging by the number of technical books written on the subject of fishing with dry flies, you would think it was the most complex form of fly fishing. But in reality, it is one of the simplest ways to take trout on a fly.

Dry flies imitate the adult stage of aquatic insects such as mayflies, stoneflies and caddisflies. Even though the adults of a particular insect appear for only a few days out of the year, you know when they're around and when trout are feeding on them because you can see the insects and watch trout taking them off the surface. It's obviously more difficult to determine what trout are eating beneath the surface.

There are times, however, when you could easily be fooled into thinking trout are feeding on a large, visible insect when, in fact, they're taking a much smaller one. It's important to watch closely until you're sure of their choice.

In dry-fly fishing, you not only know exactly where the fish are, you can see them take the fly. So you know when to set the hook.

But don't make the common mistake of casting to the rise. Remember that trout usually drift downstream beneath a floating insect before taking it. So if you cast to the ring left by the rise, your fly will land

The anticipation of a strike is what makes dry-fly fishing so exciting.

well downstream of the trout (opposite).

Although entire books have been written about "matching the hatch," it is seldom necessary to do the job perfectly. Trout never get a good look at a floating insect because they can't see clearly through the surface film. Consequently, a fly of approximately the same size, shape and color of the natural will usually do the job.

In most dry-fly fishing, you'll normally want to angle your casts upstream. This

way, your fly will drift naturally with the current. But when the current begins to form a downstream belly in your line, "drag" becomes a problem. Your fly will begin moving downstream faster than the current, leaving a wake that makes it look unnatural. To minimize the problem, you must learn to "mend" your line (opposite).

Even though the majority of dry-fly fishing involves casting upstream, there will be times when you'll have to cast across stream or downstream to reach rising trout. If a stream is too deep to wade, for instance, you have no choice but to make a cross-stream cast to reach trout rising on the opposite side. In these situations, it pays to learn the special casts shown on page 126. These casts also help reduce drag.

> ### Lines, Leaders and Flies
>
> Dry-fly fishing requires a floating line, usually a weight-forward or double-taper. Leaders vary in length from 7$\frac{1}{2}$ to 12 feet. The diameter of your tippet depends mainly on the size of your fly (p. 77). Most trout fishermen use dries in sizes 8 to 16, although flies as small as size 28 are available.

How Trout Rise to a Fly

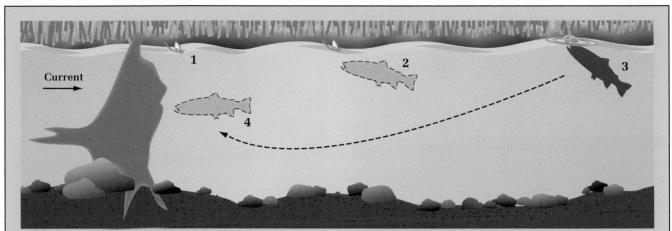

When a trout (1) spots a floating insect, it (2) drifts downstream tailfirst to examine it. After drifting from a few to more than 20 feet, the trout (3) rises to take the insect, making a ring on the surface. Then the fish quickly (4) returns to its lie. For the dry-fly fisherman, this means you must drop your fly well upstream of any rise you spot.

Popular Dry Flies

Black Elk Hair Caddis

Yellow Humpy

Tan X-Caddis

Royal Wulff

Light Cahill

Blue Wing Olive

PMD Comparadun

Black Gnat

Quill Gordon

Oliver Spinner

Royal Coachman

Mahogany Spinner

How to Mend Line

As your fly is drifting downstream, the current may begin to put a belly in your line, causing drag.

Mend the line with a flip of the rod tip, throwing a belly of line upstream. Mend the line as often as necessary during the drift.

The Reach Cast. *Strip off some line and let it hang from your reel before starting a cross-stream overhead cast. Hold the line against the rod as you cast and, while your line is still in the air, point your rod upstream (left), letting the slack shoot through the guides. When your line lands on the water, it should have a distinct upstream belly (right), which will delay the onset of drag.*

The Wiggle Cast. *Strip off some line and let it hang from your reel before starting a downstream overhead cast. While your line is still in the air, shake the rod rapidly from side to side while allowing the slack line to shoot through the guides (left). The line should have distinct curves when it lands (right), allowing the fly to drift downstream much longer before drag sets in.*

How to Keep a Dry Fly Floating

Rub floatant on your fly, especially on the hackle and tail, to keep it floating high in the water.

If your fly has absorbed too much water to float properly, rub it with a dessicant powder. Then blow off the powder and apply floatant. You can also dry your fly by making a series of false casts.

Tips for Fishing Dry Flies

Current

To imitate an emerging insect attempting to take flight, hold your rod tip high and shake it as you strip in line. This technique, called "dapping," makes the fly skip erratically on the surface.

Avoid casting straight upstream because your line will drift over the trout and possibly spook it before your fly arrives. If you must cast upstream, use a reach cast (opposite).

WET-FLY FISHING

As its name suggests, a wet fly is meant to be fished "wet," or beneath the surface.

Wets are the oldest type of fly and have been popular for centuries. And even though they are now used less often than most other types of subsurface flies, they still have a place in modern fly fishing.

Unlike nymphs and streamers, wet flies are not meant to imitate any specific food item. Some generally resemble drowned insects, insect larvae, leeches or small minnows; others are simply attractors, relying on bright colors and flash to draw strikes.

The "generic" nature of wet flies makes fly selection much easier. A dull-colored, feather-wing wet, for example, can easily be mistaken for a dozen kinds of adult insects.

Another reason for the ongoing popularity of wet flies is the ease of fishing them. Because they are relatively small, casting them is easy. And since they are normally drifted at random in midwater, your casts need not be super-accurate.

Lines, Leaders and Flies

Depending on how deep the trout are, you can use a floating, sinking or sink-tip line, either double-taper or weight-forward. With a floating line, some anglers use a leader more than 10 feet long. But a sinking line requires a much shorter leader, usually only 3 or 4 feet, so that the line can pull the fly deep enough. Because line is not as visible beneath the surface, you can use a tippet two or three sizes heavier for wet flies than for dries. Most trout anglers use wet flies in sizes 8 to 16.

Wet fly bodies are usually made of soft, absorbent materials like wool and chenille, so they sink easily. The feather or hair wings are generally swept back, offering little water resistance and giving the fly a "drowned" look.

One type of wet fly that has become a real favorite, especially among western anglers, is the wooly worm. Wound with hackle over the entire length of the body, these flies are effective because of their lifelike "breathing" action.

Some wet flies come with weighted bodies, which make it easier to get down in a deep run or pool. Another

Popular Wet Flies

Hare's Ear Soft Hackle Orange Soft Hackle Comet Boss Black Gnat

Olive Wooly Worm Black Wooly Worm Silver Doctor March Brown Light Hendrickson

way to get down more quickly is to add a split shot or two a few inches up your leader.

Exactly how you fish a wet fly depends on what you're attempting to imitate.

To mimic a drowned insect, fish the fly on a drag-free drift, as you would a dry fly. To simulate a minnow, strip in line to give the fly an erratic darting action.

How to Drift a Wet Fly

Drift

Current

Cast across stream or slightly upstream, then follow the line with your rod tip as the fly drifts. Mend line as needed to minimize drag (p. 125). Always work the water closest to you first; farthest, last. The fish may strike anywhere on the drift, but they most often take the fly at the downstream end of the drift, just as the line begins to straighten (arrow), causing the fly to change direction. After working the run, move downstream a few steps and repeat the procedure.

STREAMER FISHING

When you consider that baitfish comprise a major part of the diet of most big trout, it's not surprising that these minnow-imitating flies are so popular among trophy hunters.

Streamers are tied on extra-long hooks and have long hair or feather wings. The hooks are heavy, so they sink rapidly and will stand up to the power of a hefty trout.

Most streamers do not imitate any specific type of baitfish. They draw a trout's attention because of their color, flash and darting action.

One of the most popular types of streamers, however, does bear a close resemblance to real food. The muddler, which has a large head made of clipped deer hair, is the same shape and color as a sculpin, a favorite food of large trout.

Because of their large size, streamers create a lot of vibration. Consequently, trout can detect them using their lateral-line sense, even at night or

> ### Lines, Leaders and Flies
>
> You can fish streamers with a floating, sinking or sink-tip line. A double-taper will work in most situations, but you'll need a weight-forward line for punching these big, air-resistant flies into the wind. Use the same type of leader as you would for wet-fly fishing. Most trout anglers use streamers in sizes 1/0 to 12, along with 0X to 3X tippets.

in discolored water. Unlike flies that imitate adult insects, streamers work well almost any time of the year, even when the water is cold.

Streamers are fished in much the same way as wet flies (p. 129),

but most anglers use longer, faster strips to create a more intense darting action. This rapid retrieve makes it possible to cover the water quickly.

In cold water, however, you may have to retrieve more slowly.

For fishing in deep water or fast current, choose a streamer with lead wire wrapped around the body. Or, add some leader wrap or a split shot a few inches above the fly.

Streamers account for more trophy trout than any other type of fly.

Streamer-Fishing Tips

Choose a streamer with a mono weedguard when fishing in woody or weedy cover. A mono weedguard is stiff enough to prevent fouling yet it won't significantly reduce your hooking percentage.

Treat your streamer with floatant and use a "riffling hitch" (half-hitch around the body, inset) to make the fly skate at an angle to the current. The unusual action and surface disturbance often attract large trout.

Popular Streamers

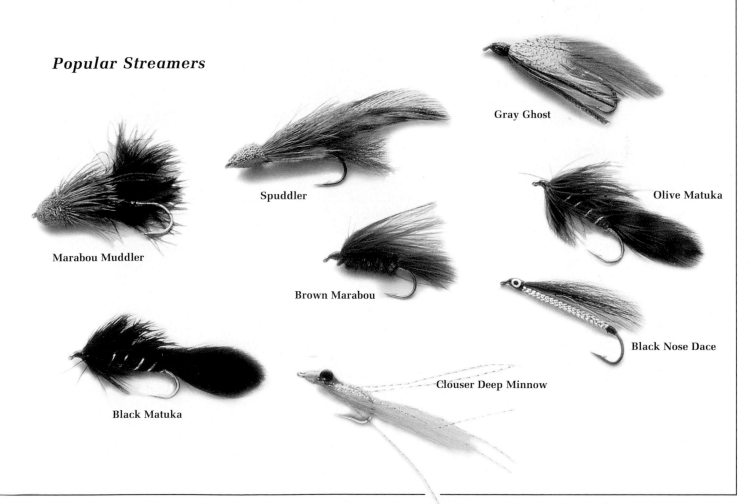

Gray Ghost

Spuddler

Olive Matuka

Marabou Muddler

Brown Marabou

Black Nose Dace

Black Matuka

Clouser Deep Minnow

NYMPH FISHING

If you could fish trout with only one type of artificial fly, your best choice—hands down—would be a nymph.

That's because nymphs imitate immature forms of aquatic insects, which are present in a stream year-round. Adult forms, in contrast, are present for only a few days out of the year. And even when the adults are hatching, trout often feed more heavily on the immature forms as they make their way toward the surface.

Nymphs are usually a better choice than wet flies because the nymphs are more realistic. Many are tied to represent specific insect types such as mayfly, stonefly, dragonfly and damselfly nymphs, as well as caddisfly larvae and pupae. Nymphs are also tied to mimic scuds. Always try to select a nymph that imitates a form present in the water you're fishing.

Arguably the most versatile type of fly, nymphs can be fished on the bottom, in midwater or in the surface film. You can also make them simulate an insect struggling toward the surface prior to hatching.

For bottom fishing, select a nymph that has lead wire wrapped around the body or a metal bead at the head for extra weight. Then angle your cast upstream far enough so the fly has a chance to sink.

To make a midwater drift, choose an unweighted nymph and cast cross-stream, just as you would with a wet fly or streamer. Let the fly drift naturally with the current, mending the line as necessary to minimize drag (p. 125).

For fishing in the surface film, you'll need an *emerger* pattern, which is tied using buoyant materials and a light hook so it barely floats. Emergers have large wing cases intended to resemble those of an insect moments away from hatching.

At times, a trout will chase an insect rising through the water while ignoring one drifting along the bottom or in midwater. To simulate a rising insect, use a technique called the "Leisenring Lift" (p. 135).

Dragonfly and damselfly imitations are usually fished by retrieving with a series of short strips to imitate the darting motion of the natural.

The most difficult part of nymph fishing is detecting the strike. Normally, all you feel when a trout takes a nymph is a slight hesitation, which doesn't feel much different from when the fly bumps a rock.

You can feel strikes more easily if you keep your casts relatively short; with a lot of line out, a subtle strike would be impossible to feel.

Instead of relying solely on feel, you can detect strikes visually by attaching a strike indicator (p. 134) to your leader.

Lines, Leaders and Flies

Fish nymphs with a weight-forward or double-taper line, either a floating, sinking or sink-tip depending on the water depth and current speed. With a floating line, use a 7½- to 12-foot leader; a sinking or sink-tip line, a 3- to 5-foot leader. Trout fishermen normally use nymphs in sizes 6 to 18, along with 2X to 7X tippets.

Popular Nymphs

Gold Bead Stone

Innis Stone

Hare's Ear (natural)

Hare's Ear (black)

Beadhead Giant Stone

Beadhead Serendipity

Beadhead Hare's Ear (olive)

Pheasant Tail

Zug Bug

March Brown

Flash Back Adams

Prince Nymph

Dragonfly Nymph

Peeking Caddis

Kauffman's Stone

Fishing with a Strike Indicator

Accomplished fly anglers often look down their noses at anyone who uses strike indicators, likening them to glorified bobbers. But strike indicators give you a definite edge, especially when you're drifting a weighted nymph along the bottom or using a split shot or leader wrap (opposite) to get down.

Indicator-fishing works best for fishing a long run with a fairly consistent depth of no more than 4 feet and a moderate current. If the water is too fast, you won't be able to keep the fly on the bottom.

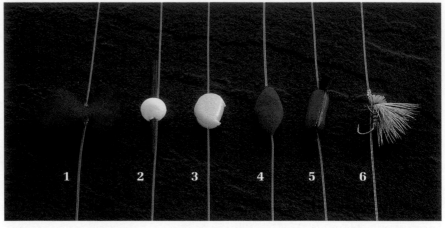

Popular strike indicators include (1) fluorescent yarn tied into the blood knot connecting leader sections; (2) styrofoam float pegged on with toothpick; (3) adhesive foam tab that pinches onto your line; (4) float putty, which can be molded around your leader; (5) slotted, twist-on type, which can be put on or taken off without removing the fly and (6) dry fly spliced into your leader.

Current

Angle your cast upstream and then allow your nymph to drift freely with the current. If you notice drag on your indicator (inset), your nymph is not drifting freely. This could be a signal to mend the line (p. 125) or it could mean that you're using too much weight. Make whatever adjustment is needed to keep the nymph drifting freely, and set the hook whenever the indicator jerks or hesitates.

The Leisenring Lift

Position yourself cross-stream of a trout's lie and then cast your nymph far enough upstream that it has time to sink before reaching the lie. As the nymph approaches the lie, stop the rod and lift it slightly. The nymph will then start to rise (arrow), imitating an immature insect swimming to the surface.

Nymph-Fishing Tips

 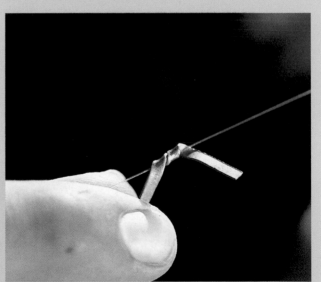

To keep your nymph floating just beneath the surface, rub fly floatant on all but the last few inches of your leader. A nymph floating in this manner represents an insect preparing to hatch.

Use a twist-on leader wrap rather than split shot, when fishing nymphs on a snaggy bottom. The lead strips, which come in a matchbook dispenser, are not as likely to hang up.

FISHING WITH SPECIALTY FLIES

Inventive fly tiers have devised patterns that represent most anything a trout could possibly eat, including leeches, crayfish, mice, salmon eggs and a variety of terrestrial insects. These "specialty flies" do not fit into any traditional fly category but there are times when they are even more effective than the usual offerings.

During a heavy grasshopper hatch, for example, it's hard to beat a "hopper" pattern. When salmon are spawning in coastal streams, try an egg fly.

Shown on these pages are the most popular types of specialty flies, along with some pointers on how to fish them.

Cricket

Black Ant

Cinnamon Ant

Beetle

Grasshopper

Terrestrials

Fly patterns have been devised to imitate grasshoppers, crickets, jassids, ants, beetles and many other kinds of terrestrial insects. Although most terrestrials are tied in sizes 8 to 20, cricket and hopper flies may be as large as size 4.

Fish most terrestrials on the surface, with a dead drift, just as you would fish a dry fly. They work best in the hottest part of the summer.

A big brown trout will seldom turn down a well-presented crayfish fly.

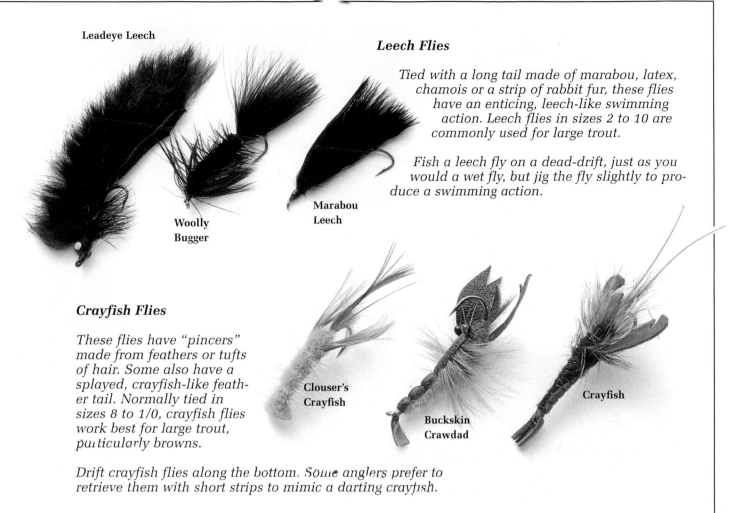

Leadeye Leech

Woolly Bugger

Marabou Leech

Leech Flies

Tied with a long tail made of marabou, latex, chamois or a strip of rabbit fur, these flies have an enticing, leech-like swimming action. Leech flies in sizes 2 to 10 are commonly used for large trout.

Fish a leech fly on a dead-drift, just as you would a wet fly, but jig the fly slightly to produce a swimming action.

Crayfish Flies

These flies have "pincers" made from feathers or tufts of hair. Some also have a splayed, crayfish-like feather tail. Normally tied in sizes 8 to 1/0, crayfish flies work best for large trout, particularly browns.

Clouser's Crayfish

Buckskin Crawdad

Crayfish

Drift crayfish flies along the bottom. Some anglers prefer to retrieve them with short strips to mimic a darting crayfish.

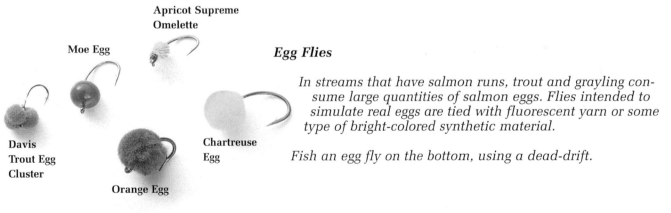

Apricot Supreme Omelette

Moe Egg

Davis Trout Egg Cluster

Orange Egg

Chartreuse Egg

Egg Flies

In streams that have salmon runs, trout and grayling consume large quantities of salmon eggs. Flies intended to simulate real eggs are tied with fluorescent yarn or some type of bright-colored synthetic material.

Fish an egg fly on the bottom, using a dead-drift.

Hair "Bugs"

Used primarily for bass and pike, hair bugs also work well for large trout. They're especially effective for fishing browns at night. Most bugs have a body of clipped deer hair and are intended to imitate mice or frogs. The most popular sizes are 4 and 6.

Fish bugs on the surface with a drag-free drift or retrieve with short twitches.

Diver

Hair Bug

A clear plastic casting bubble is difficult for trout to see in moving water.

FLY-FISHING WITH SPINNING GEAR

You don't have to be an experienced fly fisherman to catch trout on a fly. For some types of fly fishing, you can get by with light spinning tackle. Subsurface flies, including wets, nymphs and streamers, can easily be cast with spinning gear if you add a little weight a few inches up your leader.

If you don't want to weight your fly, you can fish it behind a cast-ing bubble, which is a clear float you can partly fill with water to add weight. When fished properly, the bubble is relatively inconspicuous, so it will not spook trout. Any kind of fly, either floating or sinking, can be fished on a bubble rig.

If you don't have a casting bubble, you can substitute a small styrofoam peg float or just tie a small stick to your line for extra weight.

The trick to fishing a bubble rig is to keep the fly floating downstream ahead of the bubble. If the bubble drifts over the fish before the fly arrives, it may spook them.

It's also important to cast the bubble rig well upstream of a suspected lie. A bubble splashing down right over a fish will send it scurrying for cover.

> ### Recommended Tackle
>
> For casting weighted flies, use a light spinning rod, at least 7 feet long, with a soft tip. A stiff rod will not flex enough to "load" with so little weight. Pair this with a small spinning reel spooled with limp 2- to 6-pound mono. For casting flies on a bubble rig, you can get by with a slightly heavier spinning outfit and 4- to 8-pound mono.

How to Use a Casting Bubble

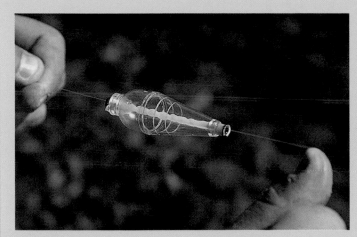

1 *Thread a casting bubble onto your line, sliding it up the line about 2 feet and then twisting the ends to lock it in place.*

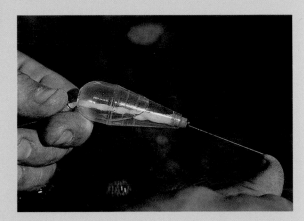

2 *If you need extra weight for casting, push the bubble under the surface and allow a little water to flow in before twisting the ends.*

Current

3 *As the bubble and fly start to drift, hold the bubble back a little to make sure the fly leads the way as the rig drifts downstream.*

4 *To get your fly deeper, fill the bubble completely with water so that it will sink.*

RELEASING TROUT

For most serious stream-trout anglers, catch-and-release has become the rule, rather than the exception. They may keep an occasional trout for a meal, but the majority are returned to fight another day.

The growing catch-and-release ethic pays big dividends, especially in heavily-fished streams near urban areas. Angler surveys consistently reveal that most of the released trout survive and are caught again, often several more times.

There is also a growing trend toward mandatory catch-and-release regulations or special size limits that require anglers to release some of their fish. For these regulations to be successful, however, you must know how to handle and release your fish properly.

If you plan to release your trout, it's a good idea to file off or flatten the barb on your hook. This way you won't have to overhandle the fish to get the hook out. Many anglers are reluctant to flatten the barb because they're afraid of losing the fish. But if you keep your line tight, the fish will rarely shake loose.

Should a fish swallow your bait or lure, don't shove a pair of pliers down its throat to remove the hook. Instead, cut the leader. Studies have shown that cutting the leader on a deep-hooked fish increases its chances for survival by about 5 times; the hook will just dissolve after awhile.

To minimize handling, use a hemostat or needle-nose pliers to unhook the fish. If you must grab the fish with your hands, be sure to wet them first. Otherwise you'll remove the trout's protective slime.

Net the fish as soon as possible. If you fight it until it is tired enough that you can land it by hand, its chances for survival diminish because of lactic acid build-up in the blood.

Don't use lures with treble hooks if you plan to release your fish. Trebles take much longer to remove and increase the odds of seriously injuring the fish.

If the fish doesn't dart off immediately, gently cradle it in your hands and keep its head facing into the current. Hold it upright until it gains the strength to swim away.

OUT OF THE ORDINARY

*T*here will be times when the usual techniques just won't do the job; then, you can open up this special bag of tricks.

Trout: Stream-Fishing Strategies

FISHING BIG WATER

Big rivers hold big trout, but you may have difficulty getting your lure to the fish. The best pools and runs are often in the middle of the river and can only be reached with a boat or a lengthy cast.

Hardware fishermen use long-handled rods for extra casting leverage. Or they attach a side-planer to their line to carry their lure into water they can't reach by casting.

Fly fishermen commonly "shoot line" to increase their casting distance (below). A shooting-head line is recommended, but you can shoot any kind of fly line. Expert casters can shoot line well over 100 feet.

Another specialized fly-casting technique, called the "double haul" (p. 146), greatly increases your line speed, resulting in considerably longer casts.

Fly casting is tough with a strong cross wind, but you can dramatically improve your casting distance by using the "reverse" cast (p. 147).

How to Shoot Line

1 Begin the cast as you would a normal overhead cast (p. 123), but gradually increase the length of your forward and backward rod strokes while false casting.

2 Before making the final forward stroke, strip off some extra line and hold it in your hand. Do not allow the extra line to trail in the water.

3 Make a final "power stroke," releasing the line and allowing it to flow through the gap between your thumb and index finger, as shown.

4 Use a stripping basket when making very long casts. This way, the excess line will not fall to the water where you would have trouble picking it up on the power stroke.

1 *Begin the cast as you would a normal overhead cast but, as you are propelling line into the backcast, use your line hand to make a smooth downward pull or "haul" about 6 inches in length (arrow). This short haul speeds up your backcast.*

2 *After the haul, bring your line hand back up to its original position as the backcast unrolls behind you.*

3 *On the forward stroke, make another haul (arrow) to maximize line speed.*

4 *After the second haul, immediately return your line hand to its original position. If desired, you can shoot line while making a double haul, further increasing casting distance.*

The "Reverse" Cast

When there is a strong cross wind coming from your rod side, the wind will blow the fly line back over your head, making casting nearly impossible. To solve the problem, turn your body 180 degrees; this way, the wind will blow the line away from you.

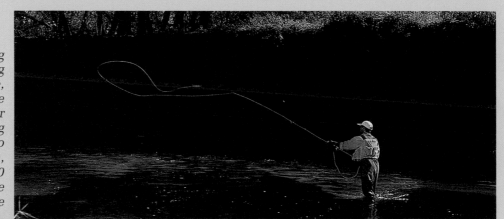

Make several false casts to get the desired amount of line into the air. Then, after the final forward cast, turn around and guide the "backcast" toward its target.

More Distance-Casting Tips

Use an extra-long rod with a two-handed grip for "power-casting" in big rivers. Some anglers use spey rods, which are up to 15 feet in length. Not only does a long rod give you extra casting leverage, it gives you stronger long-distance hooksets.

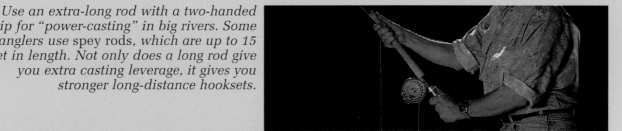

Aim your forward cast higher than normal to get maximum distance with fly-casting gear. The extra angle can increase the length of your cast by 10 to 20 feet.

A short fly rod, no more than 7 feet in length, is ideal for narrow, brush-lined trout streams.

FISHING TIGHT SPOTS

Many small trout streams have so much vegetation along the banks that you can't use the normal fly-casting methods. And even on larger streams, there will be times when you'll have to modify your casting techniques to put your fly into a tight spot.

By using a sidearm (rather than overhead) casting stroke, for example, you can place your fly under a branch or other object dangling only inches above the water. Such precision would be nearly impossible using spinning or baitcasting gear. Side-casting also helps keep your backcast under tree limbs, and the low line angle reduces the chances of spooking fish.

A steep streambank presents serious problems for fly-casters because it is impossible to make a backcast. Using the roll-casting technique, however, you can cast up to 40 feet with no backcast at all. See how to roll-cast on the next page.

You can also avoid trees, brush and other obstructions behind you (if they aren't too high) by simply elevating the plane of your backcast.

The Roll Cast

1 With the line on the water in front of you, lift your rod until it is just behind you and the line has stopped moving.

2 Make a short forward stroke, gradually increasing the speed. Stop the rod; the line will roll out in an elliptical loop and then straighten out in front of you.

Adjusting Your Casting Stroke

Side-cast to get your line beneath tree limbs or other overhanging obstacles. The casting motion is identical to that of an overhead cast, but you keep your rod moving parallel to the water's surface. This way your casting loops will be on a horizontal, rather than vertical, plane.

To avoid trees or other obstacles to your rear, elevate your backcast by moving your wrist and forearm on a tilted, rather than level, plane. An elevated backcast will shorten your forward cast, however.

TROPHY FISHING

Even streams that see a great deal of fishing pressure usually hold a few trophy-caliber trout—fish that have managed to outwit anglers for years. Many of these trout die of old age.

But don't get the idea that catching these fish is impossible. You can greatly increase your odds by following these rules:

• Fish the deepest pools, runs and undercuts. Big trout prefer deeper water than small ones, and generally hold near the bottom.

• Unlike smaller trout, big trout are not "chasers." You'll have to place your bait close to them to draw a strike.

• Large trout, especially browns and rainbows, are surprisingly tolerant of warm, discolored water. Consequently, they are often found in the muddy lower reaches of a stream, miles below the prime trout water.

• As trout grow larger, their diet generally includes a larger percentage of baitfish and a smaller percentage of insects. This explains why hardware fishermen seeking trophy trout often throw large minnowbaits and why fly fishermen rely on big streamers.

• In heavily-fished streams where trophy trout have seen every imaginable artificial

lure, your chances are best with natural bait, particularly if it is indigenous to the stream. Baits such as chubs (live or cut bait), crayfish, waterworms, hellgrammites, nightcrawlers and salmon eggs are proven big-trout producers.

• If you're intent on catching a trophy, do your fishing on streams with a history of producing numbers of big trout. As a rule, your odds are best in large, fertile streams with relatively light fishing pressure.

Popular Lures for Trophy Trout

Original
Floating Rapala

Mepps
Aglia
Spinner

Black Stone Fly

Clouser
Minnow

Blue Fox
Pixee Spoon

Muddler Minnow

Tips for Finding Trophy Trout

Deepest Pools. Look for big trout in the deepest pools, such as those that form along outside bends or at the base of a waterfall.

Logjams. Dense, woody cover, such as a logjam, offers shade and overhead protection, and provides shelter from the current.

Downstream Reaches. Although the downstream reaches of most streams hold fewer trout, they often produce the largest fish because of the warmer water and ample minnow supply.

NIGHT FISHING

Anglers who specialize in catching trophy browns know that the fish are much less cautious after dark. Instead of holing up in heavy cover, as they normally do during the day, they move into riffles and onto shallow flats where they feed aggressively. Other kinds of trout may feed after dark from time to time, but none are as active at night as the brown.

Night fishing is most productive in summer, when daytime water temperatures are above 70°F. At that time the water is normally low and clear and the fish are extra wary. Trout are even more prone to night feeding in streams that are heavily fished.

Before stumbling over rocks and logs or plowing through head-high nettles to reach a stream after dark, do some scouting in daylight to find the best path down to the water. Study each spot you plan to fish and form a mental map of the bottom. Also take note of any branches or other obstacles that may interfere with your casting.

Any of the big-trout lures shown on page 151 will work for night fishing, but remember that the fish are likely to be in shallow water. Instead of a sinking minnowbait, for example, you'll probably want to use a floater. Fly fishermen often use large, bushy dry flies that imitate mice or frogs.

Because the fish are so aggressive after dark, live bait is seldom necessary. Nor does your presentation have to be as delicate. During the day, a fly or other lure splashing down on the water will send the trout scurrying for cover; but at night, the sound may attract them.

It's a good idea to use heavier-than-normal lines and leaders at night. The fish are not as line-shy as they are during the day, so you'll get just as many strikes. But you'll lose fewer fish because of break-offs and, should you hang up in the brush while casting, a sharp jerk will usually free your lure.

Night-Fishing Tips

Use a gooseneck light that clips to your vest, for tying knots and unhooking fish after dark.

A light-colored fly is much easier to see at night than a dark one. The exact color is usually not important to the fish because all they see is the silhouette.

Other Tips for Catching Trophy Trout

Tie a large streamer upside down when fishing in heavy cover. The upturned hook is much less likely to snag, and the wing acts as a brushguard.

Let the current carry your spinner or spoon beneath an undercut bank or crib shelter. Cast upstream of the under-cut, tighten your line and allow the lure swing under the bank (dotted line).

Current

INDEX

A

Accessories, 83–86
Angler surveys, 140
Aquatic insects, 14–15, 30, 105
Arctic char, 8, 33, 46–47
  differences between Dolly
    Varden trout and, 46
  feeding habits of, 47
  habitat of, 46
  size of, 47
  water temperature preferences
    of, 47
Arctic grayling, 48–49
  feeding habits of, 48–49
  habitat of, 48
  life span of, 48
  water temperature preferences
    of, 48
Atlantic salmon, 8

B

Backtrolling, 96–97
Bait. *See* Natural bait
Baitcasting reels
  capacity, 73
  drag, 73
  level-wind, 73
Baitcasting rods
  action, 73
  handle, 73
  length, 73
  power, 73
Baitfish, 16
Basic fly casting, 122–123
Bell Island (Alaska), 25
Big rivers, fishing in, 145–149
Boats and motors, 80–81
Bob Marshall Wilderness, 43
Brook trout, 8, 32–35, 37
  feeding habits of, 13, 32
  habitat of, 32
  hybridization of, 34
  size of, 32
  spawning habits of, 34
  water temperature
    preferences, 33–34
Brown trout, 7–8, 28–31, 150

feeding habits of, 13, 30
habitat of, 28, 30–31
lake dwelling, 30
life span of, 30
markings of, 29
subspecies of, 28–29
trophy, 152
Bull trout, 8, 33, 42–43
  feeding habits of, 13, 42–43
  habitat of, 43
  life span of, 43
  main differences between
    Dolly Varden trout and, 43
  spawning habits of, 43
  water temperature preferences
    of, 43

C

Caddisflies, 15, 30
Casting angle, determining, 94
Casting bubble, 71, 139
Casting stroke, adjusting, 149
Catch-and-release fishing, 9, 140
Char, 8. *See also* Arctic char
Chubs, 16
Clark's Fork River (Montana), 31
Coastal cutthroat trout, 38–39
Coastal streams, 61
Coasters, 35
Corkie, 113
Crankbaits, 93
Crayfish, 17
Crayfish flies, 137
Crib shelters, 63, 65
Cricket dispenser, 109
Crickets, 105
Cross-stream cast, 124, 129
Crustaceans, 106
Current seams, 65
Cutthroat trout, 25, 36–39
  feeding habits of, 13
  habitat preferences of, 37
  life span of, 37–38
  spawning habits of, 37
  subspecies of, 36
  water temperature preferences
    of, 36

D

Dabbling, 116
Dac11.047e, 16
Deep pools, 65
Deep slot, 65
Distance-casting tips, 147
Dolly Varden trout, 33, 43–45
  differences between Arctic
    char and, 46
  feeding habits of, 13, 45
  habitat of, 44
  main differences between bull
    trout and, 43
  size of, 44–45
  spawning habits of, 44
Double-clinch (Trilene) knot, 121
Double haul, 145–146
Double-taper lines (DT), 75
Downstream trolling, 96
Dragonfly and damselfly imita-
  tions, 133, 135
Drift-fishing, 110–111, 113
  recommended tackle, 111
Drifting, 95, 100
Drop-back technique, 96–97
Dry-fly fishing, 76, 124–127
  lines, leaders and flies, 124
  special casts for, 126

E

Eddies, 65
Egg clusters-spawn bag and egg
  loop, 107
Egg flies, 137
Egg loop, 107
Endangered Species List, 42

F

Feeding habits, 13–19
  aquatic insects, 14–15
  of Arctic char, 47
  of Arctic grayling, 48–49
  baitfish, 16
  of brook trout, 13, 32
  of brown trout, 13, 30
  of bull trout, 13, 42–43
  of cutthroat trout, 13
  of Dolly Varden trout, 13, 45
  of golden trout, 41

of trout, 13–19
Fishing vest, 83
Floater, 113
Floating, 114
   tips, 115
Floating lines (F), 75, 124
Floating/sinking lines (FS), 75
Fluorocarbon leader material, 76
Fly casting, 122-123, 145
Fly fisherman, 7
Fly fishing, 118–139
   basic casting, 122–123
   dry, 124–127
   nymph, 132–135
   recommended tackle, 138
   specialty flies, 136–137
   streamer, 130–131
   tackle, 120–121
   wet, 128–129
   with spinning gear, 138–139
Fly leaders, 76–77
Fly line, 74–75
Fly reels
   material, 70
   size/capacity, 70
   type of action, 70
   type of drive, 70
Fly rods, 69
   action, 69
   length, 69
   material, 69
   weight, 69
Fly size versus tippet diameter,
   77
Fly tackle, rigging, 120–121
Foothill streams, 59
Freelining, 111–112
Freestone streams, 57, 59
French spinners, 91

G

German brown trout, 28
Glacier National Park, 43
Golden trout, 40–41
   color markings of, 40–41
   feeding habits of, 41
   habitat of, 40–41
   hybridization of, 41
   size of, 41
   spawning habits of, 41
GoreTex wading gear, 79
Grasshoppers, 105
Grayling, 8, 21

Great Lakes tributaries, 27
Grocery/prepared baits, 106

H

Hair bugs, 137
Hardware, fishing with, 90–99
Hatch chart, 18
Heavily-fished streams, 150
Hotshotting, 96
Hybridization
   of brook trout, 34
   of golden trout, 41
   of rainbow trout, 25

I

Indicator-fishing, 134
Inflatable rafts, 80–81
In-line spinners, 91
   recommended tackle, 91
Insects, 13
   aquatic, 14–15, 30, 105
   terrestrial, 17, 105, 136

J

Jet boats, 80–81
Jewel Lake (British Columbia),
   25
Jig fishing, 100–101
   lures, 101
   recommended tackle, 100

K

Kern River trout, 40
Knotless leaders, 76
Knotted leaders, 76
Kype, 21, 30

L

Lahontan cutthroat trout, 38–39
Lake trout, 33
Large-lake tributaries, 61

Leeches, 17
Leech flies, 137
"Leisenring Lift," 133, 135
Level lines (L), 75
Lie, 31
Limestone streams, 57–58
Lines, 74
   buoyancy, 75
   fly, 74–75
   fly leaders, 76–77
   spinning and baitcasting, 75
   taper, 75
   weight, 74–75
Little Red River (Arkansas), 29
Live bait
   popular types of, 104–107
   tips for carrying and keeping,
     109
   tips for catching, 108
Loch Leven trout, 28
Loop knot, 121
Loop-to-loop connection, 121
Lures for trophy fishing, 151

M

Mashutuk River (Alaska), 45
Matching the hatch, 124
Mayflies, 14, 18, 30
McKenzie River boat, 80, 95
Meadow streams, 60
Meandering stream, 55, 64
Meltwater, 53
Mending line, 124–125
Midges, 15
Minnowbaits, 93
Minnows, 104
Mock spawning run, 27
Mountain streams, 59

N

Natural bait, fishing with,
   103–117
Neoprene wading gear, 78
Night fishing, 152–153
Nylon wading gear, 78
Nymph fishing, 132–135
   lines, leaders and flies, 133

O

Overhead cast, 123

P

Pacific salmon, 8, 26
Perfection loop, 120
Plugs, recommended tackle, 93
Pool-riffle-run configuration, 55–56
Put-and-take lakes, 25
Pyramid Lake (Nevada), 38

R

Rainbow trout, 7–9, 24–27, 150
    habitat of, 25
    hybridization of, 25
    life span of, 25
    size of, 25
    spawning habits of, 25
    subspecies of, 25
Reach cast, 126
"Reading the water," 62–65
Red-band rainbow trout, 25
Redds
    for bull trout, 43
    construction of, 21
Reels
    fly, 70
    spinning, 72
Reverse cast, 145, 147
Riffle, 55
Rods
    baitcasting, 73
    fly, 69
    spinning, 71
Roll cast, 149
Rubber wading gear, 79
Run, 55

S

Salmon family, 8
Salters, 35
Scuds, 17
Sculpins, 16
Sea trout, 31, 35
Shiners, 16

Shooting-head line, 145
Shooting-taper lines (ST), 75
Shoot line, 145
Sidearm, 148
Side-casting, 148
Side-planers, 98–99, 145
Single salmon eggs, 106
Sinking lines (S), 75, 128
Sink-tip lines, 75
Slipping, 96
Slip-sinker rig, 116
Small trout streams, fishing, 148–149
Sonic spinners, 91
Spawn bag, 107
Spawning cycle, stages of, 23
Spawning habits, 9, 20–23
    of brook trout, 34
    of bull trout, 43
    of cutthroat trout, 37
    of Dolly Varden trout, 44
    of golden trout, 41
    of rainbow trout, 25
Specialty flies, fishing with, 136–137
Speckled trout, 32
Spinning and baitcasting lines, 75
Spinning gear, fly-fishing with, 138–139
Spinning reels
    drag, 72
    shape of spool, 72
    size, 72
Spinning rods
    action, 71
    length, 71
    material, 71
    power, 71
Splake (speckled X lake), 34
Split-shot rig, 116
Spoons, recommended tackle, 92
Spring creeks, 58
Standing wave forms, 64
Steelhead, 25–26
    summer versus winter runs, 26–27
Still-fishing
    recommended tackle, 116
    tips for, 117
Stocking-foot, 79
Stoneflies, 15, 30
Streamer fishing, 130–131
    lines, leaders and flies, 130
Stream-fishing techniques, 87–141

Stream trout, 9
Strike indicator, fishing with, 134
Summer-run, 26

T

Tailwater streams, 60
Terrestrial insects, 17, 105, 136
Tiger trout, 29, 34
Tippet diameter, 76
    versus fly size, 77
Tree River (Northwest Territories), 47
Trolling, 96–97
Trolling plugs, 93
Trophy fishing, 150–153
    for bull trout, 42–43
    tackle for, 151
Trout
    basics in fishing for, 7–9
    feeding habits, 13–19
    releasing, 140–141
    senses, 10–11
    smell of, 11
    spawn habits of, 9
    tips for approaching, 88–89
    vision of, 10–11
    and water movement, 9
Trout eggs, 22
Trout habitat, 53
    gradient, 54
    shade, 57
    shape of streambed, 54–55
    water fertility, 57
    water temperature preferences, 4, 8, 33–34, 36, 43, 47, 53–54
Trout streams, types of, 58–61
True trout, 8
Tube knot, 120
Twitch-and-pause, 100

U

Underground springs, 53
Upstream trolling, 96

V

Vertical jigging, 100

W

Waders and hip boots, 78–79
   materials, 78
   sole type, 78
   style, 78
Wading, 94
Water, reading, 62–65
Water temperature preferences,
   8, 53–54
   for Arctic char, 47
   for brook trout, 33–34
   for bull trout, 43
   for cutthroat trout, 36
Water tumbling, 64
Waterworm, 105
Weight-forward lines (WF), 75
West Slope cutthroat trout,
   37–39
Wet-fly fishing, 128–129
   lines, leaders and flies, 128
White, Stewart Edward, 41
Whitefish, 8
Wiggle cast, 126
Wildlife Forever, 35
Winter-run, 26–27
Wooly worm, 129
Worms, 104

Y

Yarn fly, 112
Yellowstone cutthroat trout, 39